*To:*_____

*From:*_____

THE WHOLE HEART OF

I CHING

THE CHINESE BOOK OF CHANGES FROM THE ORAL TRADITION

CRANE HILL
PUBLISHERS

ISBN-13: 978-1-57587-280-3

Printed in China

Library of Congress Cataloging-in-Publication Data

Bright-Fey, J. (John)
  The Whole heart of *I Ching* : the complete teachings from the Chinese book
of changes / Bright-Fey, John.
      p. cm.
  ISBN 978-1-57587-280-3
  1. Yi jing. I. Title. II. Title: Complete teachings from the Chinese book
of changes.

  PL2464.Z6B75 2008
  299'.51282–dc22

2007018321

THE WHOLE HEART OF

I CHING

THE CHINESE BOOK OF CHANGES
FROM THE ORAL TRADITION

REVEREND VENERABLE
JOHN BRIGHT-FEY

CRANE HILL
PUBLISHERS

DEDICATION

For Professor Chung So
Poet, Teacher, Friend

Thanks for the advice.
I'm very glad I took it.

Ch'an Sung / Deep Relaxation

TABLE OF CONTENTS

Ch'an Chih / Deep Intuition

A RICH INNER LIFE

To study the *I Ching* (pronounced Yee-Jing) is to engage in a philosophical study of human psychology as it interacts with the world. Generally speaking, it is interactive literature that is designed to challenge the democracy of our perceptions imposed by habitual structures of thought and behavior. Said another way, it allows us to see the hidden side of life.

Once the hidden side is revealed, this thoroughly amazing text suggests courses of action specifically designed to add to the richness of our existence. Events of all kinds—geography, weather, seasonal rhythms, other individuals, animal and plant life, or any phenomena that we, as human beings, encounter—can be investigated with the *I Ching* and its secrets laid bare.

In this volume, my primary focus will be to explore the traditional approach to the *I Ching* that exists within the "closed door" tradition of Taoist Masters and Disciples. "Closed Door" within the Chinese tradition identifies a transmission of wisdom and information that is private in nature. It is usually reserved for only the most gifted and trusted of initiates. Historically, this transmission has been a strictly oral affair relying upon a prodigious memory and long hours of call and response. Now, all of that is about to change.

I believe that the world at large could benefit greatly from the immeasurable wisdom and knowledge contained in the *I Ching*. Yet, so much of the conventional information previously available obscures more than it reveals. This presentation, however, is anything but conventional. I humbly offer it for your consideration and study. I hope that it opens the world for you, the way it has for me. My goal is to turn you into authentic Cultivators of this magnificent philosophical work as soon as possible.

Consulting and cultivating the *I Ching* is a way to complete ourselves, fulfill the promise of our humanity, and claim the vast Universe as our own. It is this experience of the *Book of Changes* that I can now share with you.

You are about to begin an authentic journey into the Chinese heart and Taoist soul. Along the way you will learn theory, history, technique, and mind-body skills. Each step of the journey will take you deeper into the realm of limitlessness where you will encounter the *Whole Heart of I Ching*. Welcome aboard.

John Bright-Fey
Reverend Venerable
Tao-Jen, Tao-Shih

Birmingham, Alabama
2008

THE POEM OF CHANGE

The *I Ching* as a text is a book of mystic poetry. Taoists regard it as a sacred expression recorded in the language of the infinite. This poetic language communicates its ideas in the form of images and not in prosaic descriptions.

As with poetry from all cultures, it constructs pictures in our consciousness that briefly become part of the bodymind in order to reveal its wisdom. It is a carefully constructed work of ancient metaphors and parables that, in fact, only become relevant when mystically inhabiting a bodymind. It is intimacy personified and cannot be called divination or fortune telling in the conventional sense.

The most important facet of this mystic poetry is the human element that must be poured into it. Specifically, this is the act of ritually consulting the *I Ching* as an oracle, performing the contemplations it prescribes, and following the advice it recommends. For its ancient wisdom to come alive in the present, this vital part of the equation must be properly trained.

Also, one must have access to esoteric knowledge to fully engage and benefit from the process. In other words, the poetry of our lives must meet the poetry of Eternity. This is the crux of Taoist approach.

THE SYMBOLS OF CHANGE

In addition to the ancient literary language that makes up the verse of the *Book of Changes*, the *I Ching* also contains a series of linear graphic designs made up of solid and broken lines. These lines are known as *yao* and represent specific configurations of *Qi* or life energy. A solid line represents outflowing or expanding *Yang Qi*, while a broken line is representative of inflowing or condensing *Yin Qi*. There are eight three-line kua, or trigrams, that form the basic building blocks of this graphic language.

The Eight Trigrams

They are compounded (8x8) into 64 hexagrams, or six-line figures, upon which the entire "Poem of Change" hangs. Whether composed of three or six lines, these lined graphics are called kua, which means Primal Image Symbol. Each hexagram graphically represents and records specific frequencies of life-force energy encountered by man within his Universe. This is a sophisticated and dynamic worldview that forms the warp and woof of the *I Ching*.

A Hexagram

Through the complex use of trigrams and hexagrams, the *I Ching* becomes, in point of fact, an encoded document that must be approached with a sacrifice of human energy, as that is the only means of decoding it. Taoists call this sacrifice Heng and it is central to cultivating a life informed by the *Book of Changes*.

Let me be clear; this is a direct "hands-on" approach and not a theoretical one. The Cultivator deliberately chooses a Hexagram that represents a singular moment in spacetime (see page 14 or 25), determines the critical point of the changing energies present at that moment (see page 16), determines precisely how the situation is evolving (see page 29), and sets about mystically exploring the moment (see pages 31–37). During this process, the Cultivator begins to viscerally experience the holographic interconnectedness of Creation.

When the Taoist Cultivator fully and completely brings himself to this mystic sacrifice, knowledge and insight of all kinds cascade upon him. It's as if he becomes a musical instrument, a tuning fork resonating harmonically with the music of the Tao itself. Consciousness expands, creativity is enhanced, and the talents of the bodymind become amplified as intuition, judgment, and perception increase dramatically.

Through this directed approach, Taoist Cultivators gain greater access to themselves and to the world around them, as they become Cultivators of the Universe. That is precisely what the *I Ching* is designed to provide.

Ch'an Ping / Deep Peace

CONSULTING THE
I CHING

Taoists preserve several remarkable methods of consulting the *Book of Changes*. Each relies heavily upon a uniquely Taoist worldview in which seemingly ordinary occurrences reveal extraordinary wisdom and insight into the hidden nature of the Universe. I will present two of these methods. The first will be a Sung Dynasty method involving the use of three coins. The second is called Inner World Divination and employs seemingly ordinary events in spacetime to unlock the secrets of the cosmos.

It is important to remember that when you consult the *I Ching* through either of these processes you are, in reality, asking yourself a question. Sometimes the question is obvious, such as, "Should I take the new job that was offered to me?" At other times the question itself is often vague and indistinct. Either way, the *I Ching* is a marvelous aid to decision-making because it reveals the forces of Yin and Yang at work in your personal situation no matter how confused or adrift you feel.

This is because the question isn't being put to your limited self. Rather, when consulting the oracle of the *I Ching*, you are submitting a question to your unlimited self, which is connected to the vast Universe and cosmic source known as the Tao. Both the text and the manner in which you interact with it help engineer a unique experience of spacetime as it shifts and changes around you. Each act of *I Ching* consultation becomes a soul-affirming act of empowerment in which you open yourself to the field of all possibilities and dare to glimpse your intimate connection to the workings of the Tao.

THE COIN METHOD

During the Southern Sung Dynasty (1127-1279 CE), Taoist mystics invented a quick and simple way of consulting the *I Ching*. This method involves the ritual tossing of three copper coins as a means of determining the archetypal forces at work during any given moment in spacetime.

Simply put, the tossing creates a state of randomness in which the significant forces exert themselves and shape the outcome of the coin toss. Each toss reveals either Yin (receptive) forces or Yang (creative) forces at work in the moment. Six tosses of the coins reveal an intricate pattern of energy moving beneath the surface of reality. Once you become aware of that pattern, you can shape your actions accordingly to ensure a positive end result.

Here's how it works:

1) Obtain three coins. Old pennies are best because they are made of copper, but any three similar coins will do.

2) Armed with this *I Ching*, pen, paper, and your three coins, find a place where you can focus on the procedure. You will also need a tabletop or some other working surface.

3) Calm yourself and sit quietly for a few moments. After a brief period of contemplation, begin to formulate a question to put to the Universe. Write the question down on your paper. Using eight words or less when forming your question will provide optimal results. The question can be very specific ("Should I take the new job in

Seattle?") or very general ("What life lessons should I watch for today?"). Focus on the question or inquiry until it is foremost in your bodymind.

4) Pick up the three coins and begin to shake them between your hands. Continue to think about your question as you shake the coins.

5) When it feels right, toss the coins to the table. The coins will turn up either heads, which is considered Yin with a value of 2, or tails, which is considered Yang with a value of 3. After the toss, add the values of the coins.

Your results will be
one of the following:

$$\left(\frac{HEADS}{2}\right) + \left(\frac{HEADS}{2}\right) + \left(\frac{HEADS}{2}\right) = 6$$

$$\left(\frac{HEADS}{2}\right) + \left(\frac{TAILS}{3}\right) + \left(\frac{TAILS}{3}\right) = 8$$

An even total is represented
by a broken line: ▰ ▰

$$\left(\frac{HEADS}{2}\right) + \left(\frac{HEADS}{2}\right) + \left(\frac{TAILS}{3}\right) = 7$$

$$\left(\frac{TAILS}{3}\right) + \left(\frac{TAILS}{3}\right) + \left(\frac{TAILS}{3}\right) = 9$$

An odd total is represented
by a solid line: ▬▬▬

6) Write down either a solid or broken line on your paper.

7) Pause briefly to reflect upon your question. After a period of time, pick up the three coins and repeat the process of shaking and tossing. Remember, it is during this step that the forces at work within and without you affect the outcome of the toss. After this second toss, add the values and determine the result. Write the Yin (broken-line graphic) or Yang (solid-line graphic) on top of the first. Repeat the entire process four more times until you have constructed a six-lined hexagram from the bottom up. Remember, all hexagrams are constructed from the bottom to the top.

8) Immediately after recording the sixth toss, silently make the following statements to yourself and determine which one has the most personal significance. That is, decide which statement rings truest for you at this specific moment.

1) "I am calm and relaxed."
2) "I am resolute and wholehearted."
3) "I am stable, strong, and rooted."
4) "I am focused and clear."
5) "I am giving and expressive."
6) "I am connected to my surroundings."

Make note of which number relates best to you at this moment; it will be explained later on.

9) When you have the six-lined picture graphically displaying the forces of Yin and Yang at work in your situation, turn to the locator chart in back of this book. Cross reference the top three lines (Upper trigram) with the bottom three lines (Lower trigram) in order to determine which Hexagram has been produced.

HEXAGRAM LOCATOR

Upper → Trigrams Lower ↓	Ch'ien ☰	Chên ☳	K'an ☵	Kên ☶	K'un ☷	Sun ☴	Li ☲	Tui ☱
Ch'ien ☰	1	34	5	26	11	9	14	43
Chên ☳	25	51	3	27	24	42	21	17
K'an ☵	6	40	29	4	7	59	64	47
Kên ☶	33	62	39	52	15	53	56	31
K'un ☷	12	16	8	23	2	20	35	45
Sun ☴	44	32	48	18	46	57	50	28
Li ☲	13	55	63	22	36	37	30	49
Tui ☱	10	54	60	41	19	61	38	58

**(Note: A large Hexagram Locator chart
is available on page 295)**

10) Once you know the *I Ching* Canto to consult, turn to that Canto and study its contents, follow its advice, and perform the meditations it prescribes. The next section will outline the structure of each Canto in this Taoist *I Ching* and explain how to interact with it.

THE TAOIST METHOD

The authentic Taoist method for consulting the *I Ching* is called Inner World Divination. It rests upon the symbolism of the Pa Kua or "Eight Primal Image Symbols." More commonly, they are called the Eight Trigrams. Each of these Eight Trigrams is representative of the various aspects and constituent parts of the phenomenal world as experienced by humanity. For Taoists, they are the building blocks of reality. The Eight Trigrams form a precise language necessary for a complete discussion of man's experience. Likewise, the *I Ching* forms the precise method for using this language to unlock the many mysteries of that experience.

Literally, anything can be classified according to its fundamental pattern of Qi. In a sophisticated system of correspondences that would eventually span all phases of art, science, and culture, ancient Chinese man recorded the world he encountered as an interplay of *Yin* Qi and *Yang* Qi. Over the ensuing centuries, Taoist priests preserved this data, adding to it and clarifying it as necessary.

To be a true Cultivator of the Taoist *I Ching*, it is required that you, too, become completely familiar with these building blocks. Once you are, you will begin to see the interplay of Qi all around you in the phenomenal world. Armed with this knowledge, you will be able to successfully employ Inner World Divination.

Kua Correspondences

The following charts list various phenomena and the Kua that specifically relates to them. Read and study each in great detail. It is on the shoulders of these correspondences that your entire understanding of the Taoist *I Ching* will stand. Please remember, each phenomenon listed in the charts is expressed as a pattern of energy it creates within the bodymind when it is encountered.

Kua Correspondences: Chien / Heaven

Chien People- A father, an old man; a timekeeper or referee; a boss; a general; a mechanic; an energetic or driven person; someone with foresight; policeman; an enforcer of laws and rules; a famous person; brave people; a powerful individual; tall people

Chien Places- The directions south or northwest; cold temperature places; clear and bright places; forward moving roads or paths; top of something; structures natural or man-made that frame something else; a place of natural force or overwhelming beauty; capitals; landscaped areas; public buildings

Chien Things- Horse, lion, goose, elephant; October through mid-December; circles, round; kings, rulers, presidents; jade; money, riches, precious stones, and metals; 7 pm to 10 pm; things made of metal; bones; deep red in color, dark colors in general; big cars or large conveyances; clocks and other time-keeping devices; ice; machines; the head; fruit-bearing trees; lungs; meat and fruits; the number 6; six things

Chien Ideas- Strength, strong; creativity; calculating and cold; great or grand; moving, to move; firmness; resolute; to turn or revolve; forceful expression; to bump out of the way; to meet headlong; decisiveness; bravery

Kua Correspondences: Kun / Earth

Kun People- Mothers; old women; farmers; Queen; servants; sensitives and intuitive individuals; people with common sense; plain and unadorned people; group leaders; large masses of people; shaded person; stonemason and brick layers; sickly people; patients

Kun Places- Earth; home; villages, small towns, farms and rural communities; antique stores; a field or plain; cloudy or rainy places; north to northwest or southwest in direction; open halls and empty meeting rooms; basement; small house

Kun Thing- Oxen, cows, mares, and deer; antiques, things of great age; 1 pm to 5 pm; yellow or gold in color; handles or places to grip; clouds and rain; things dark; soil; cloth; cotton and silk; November, early June, July to early September; abdomen, stomach, and flesh; empty jugs and containers; pots, cauldron; flexible things; tree trunk; the numbers 8 and 2; eight things or two things

Kun Ideas- Obedience; receptivity; to hold; to support someone or something; quietude; smooth things; visceral feelings; being down to earth; to lead away or redirect; to store away; silence; calm; passivity; peace and quiet; softness

Kua Correspondences: Ken / Mountain

Ken People- Young man, young son; youngest brother; family or families; someone to lean on for support; a counselor, lawyer; mountain climber, explorer, teenager;

vagabond; slow people; stubborn and independent individuals

Ken Places- Mountains and mountain ranges; graveyards; portals, doorways, gateways; lodges and hotels; second stories; bridges; pathways or side paths; zoo; backdoors; small or narrow roads; plateaus and vistas; cloudy and misty areas

Ken Things- Dogs; hands in general; early February, early March; northwest or northeast; gates; volcano; 1 am to 5 am; fruit; tigers, monkeys; small rocks; shoulder; a fan; things made of stone; dark yellow or burnt orange in color; things that are covered; animals with long snouts; the numbers 7 or 8; seven or eight things

Ken Ideas- To halt or stop; keeping very still and sedate; alternate paths, thinking outside the conventional; to stand one's ground; stillness; to shoulder the responsibility; indecision; to stagnate; to contradict; being independent

Kua Correspondences: Tui / Lake

Tui People- Young girls and young women, daughter, female singer, hostess, beautiful women; happy people; drummer or percussionist; prostitute; witch; gold collector; woodland guide; guides and pathfinders in general

Tui Places- Restaurant; kitchen; places that induce a pleasurable feeling; lakes and ponds; slow moving water; aviary; places to the right (as opposed to the left); southeast or west; marsh; tea house or coffee shop; wells; valley; ditches; swimming pools

Tui Things- Mouth; an opening; sword; coffee or tea; oval shaped things; birds; things that hurt or injure; elbow; closed fist; the precious metal gold; needles and things honed to a sharp point; 5 pm to 7 pm; mid-September and mid-October; sheep; abandoned and unsafe structures; horned animals; the numbers 2 or 7; two things or seven things

Tui Ideas- Joyousness, pleasure, happiness; to hurt or injure; to beat or hit something sharply; rhythm; sudden impact; restlessness; weakness; harshness; abrasiveness; fall feelings; broken promises; quarrelsome; optimism; slander and gossip

Kua Correspondences: Kan / Water

Kan People- Middle son; very respectful individuals; persons of an evil nature; a sleepy or tired person; someone exhibiting great vitality; priests and clergy; gloomy people; depressed people; presenter, host; someone jostling or shaking a person or thing; thief

Kan Places- Ditches; plowed fields; waterfalls; rivers and fast moving water; mills, harnessed water; taverns and bars; places to sleep or rest; sacred places; hazardous places; snowy places; places painted red; bathrooms; swamps

Kan Things- Traps; ear; pigs and boars; early December through early January; 10 pm to 1 am; west, south, or north in direction; wheels; clouds; snakes; manacles or restraints of any kind; fuel; kidneys; ink pens and writing implements; bow and arrow; very heavy rain; the moon; boats and ships; hail; dew; the number 6; six things

Kan Idea- To entrap something; to menace; devilishness; to energize or fuel; danger, warning; mental distress or anxiety; to show great respect; perilous; to shake things up; cunning; deceit; to steal something; sadness and melancholy; disturbing

Kua Correspondences: Li / Fire

Li People- Middle daughter; teachers; artists; librarians; doctors, nurses, and healers; conmen; fiery personalities; optimistic individuals; someone pushing a person or thing; agitated people; students; military personnel; enlightened people; wise people; dedicated people

Li Places- Churches, temples, and places of worship; horse races; hospitals and health clinics; sunsets and sunrises; east or south; land blighted by drought; sunny and bright places; empty buildings; building with lots of windows; places of safety; round empty areas

Li Things- Fire; pheasants, wild birds; eyes; bright red things; firearms; the sun; lightning; spears and swords; protective armor; protective helmet; crab, horses; early June through early July; 11 am to 1 pm; medical procedures; push with two hands; things round and empty; the numbers 3 and 9; three things or nine things

Li Ideas- Magnificence; clarity; brightness; to catch or seize; strong outside but weak inside; to burn; alchemic transformation; trial by fire; to sharply and critically reason; happiness and the sounds of happiness; to give light and comfort; hot; to surround; to claim safety; dedication and loyalty; wisdom

Kua Correspondences: Chen/ Thunder ䷲

Chen People- Eldest son; young men/man; middle-aged men (30-45); managers, controllers; mail carriers and messengers; people embracing each other; excitable individuals; music makers; angry people

Chen Places- Great roads and highways; places far away but clear in the memory; hubs of coordinated activity; bamboo gardens; northeast or east in direction

Chen Things- Thunder; dragons; feet; flowing motion; blue; radio, phone, and any device for communication over a great distance; bamboo; early March through early April; 5 am to 7 am; waves of water, motion, sound, or activity; music; the numbers 3 and 4; three things and four things

Chen Ideas- Impetus to movement or motion; drawing strength from a curve; a movement of ideas; to arouse; firmness in stance; to separate or split apart; to embrace a life situation; active; excitable; nervous or anxious; to succeed

Kua Correspondences: Sun/Wind

Sun People- Eldest daughter; young woman/women; short people, balding people; travelers; idealists; salesperson; kind and compassionate individuals; pickpockets and quick thieves; widow; nun; anyone in seclusion; excitable persons; people who are neat and tidy

Sun Places- A place you traveled to; southwest or southeast; windy places and places of a lofty setting;

airports and harbors; forests; long expanses of forest or terrain; stores and markets; garden

Sun Things- Wind and breezes; chicken; long hair; guitar and other string instruments; willow trees; things white in color; fragrant things; 7am to 11am; needle and thread; birds in flight; tree-tops; thighs and hips; long things

Sun Ideas- Penetrating strength; rocking motions; lofty ideas; gentleness; following the straight and narrow; to pluck an idea from the air; to seize something; to cultivate; yielding; weak or weakness; fragrance

Inner World Divination

Modern science has discovered that, contrary to commonly held belief, we do not actually observe our physical world. In reality, we participate in it. Through a complex series of neurological communication and feedback, our sense organs (eyes, ears, etc.) collaborate with our brain to literally create what we experience as "out there."

Interestingly enough, the ancient science of the *I Ching* tells us exactly the same thing. However, cultivators of the *Book of Changes* do not speak of sense organs and brain function. Instead, they identify the various agents and forces that co-create our reality as Qi.

The Qi that shapes our perception and comprehension of reality is called Inner World Energy. Inner World Energy is the Qi of fear, want, need, past experience, and past prejudice. It is the Qi that exists as a consequence of our corporeal existence. What we consciously think about or focus on is part of the inner world.

Our conditioned responses, habits, rationalizations, beliefs, illusions, and attachments are all part of the mix. Even the unconscious mind contributes to the landscape of the inner world. In short, the Qi of our Inner World is the sum total of our individual human gifts and deficits.

The goal of a Taoist *I Ching* Cultivator is to so thoroughly explore and understand the phenomena of the conditioned inner world of illusion that he is able to slip past it and experience the unconditioned original wonders of the Universe. This is accomplished by a directed study of the *I Ching* guided by Inner World Divination.

The Inner World Divination Process

Step 1) Inner World Divination uses everyday experiences, such as a walk in the park, as a means of determining a hexagram. The energies of the things we might experience during our walk are represented by the Eight Trigrams. Our responses to them are represented by a circular arrangement of the trigrams. This is meant to imply the constantly changing nature of existence and our responses to it. Think of these changing energies as eight different dimensions that overlap to form consensual reality. To begin the divination, imagine that you are at the intersection of these eight different dimensional energies as, in this example, you walk in the park. (See illustration, opposite page.)

Step 2) Any event in spacetime that catches and significantly holds your attention is appropriate for divination. For example, as you are walking through the park, you suddenly hear the sound of laughter coming from two people near a stand of trees just to your right. An event in spacetime has just occurred—people laughing in the park.

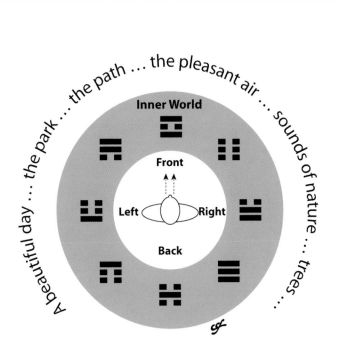

Inner World Divination- The Park

Step 3) Now, you turn to your right front in order to more clearly see where the laughter is coming from. Think of this direction as a window through which you look at the event. Expressing it in Taoist terms, you see the event through the window named *K'un* or "Earth." The direction from which the event calls your attention and flows towards you determines the bottom portion of the hexagram. (See illustration, following page.)

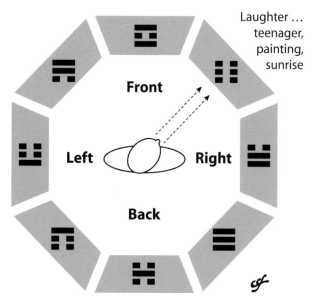

Laughter ...
teenager,
painting,
sunrise

Front

Left

Right

Back

Inner World Divination- Windows

Step 4) Immediately upon looking through your "Earth" window, you see a teenage girl receiving a lesson by an art teacher on how to paint a sunrise. There is something special about this tableau that holds your attention. Perhaps it's the painting of the sunrise itself or the teenager trying to properly hold her paintbrush that draws your interest.

Through your knowledge of the Eight Kua (or by referring to the Kua Correspondence Charts on pages 19-25) you are able to determine that teenage girls, teachers, artists, and sunrises can all be represented with the trigram Li or "Fire."

28

Use this trigram to form the top part of your hexagram. Utilizing the cross-reference chart you find the thirty-fifth hexagram called Chin, Progress/Advance/Flourish. This is your *Pen Kua* or "Original Hexagram." It is your unique moment in the park expressed in the ancient language of the *I Ching*.

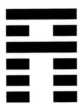

Hexagram 35
Chin
Progress/Advance/Flourish

Step 5) Silently repeat the six statements on page 16 and choose the one that most resonates with you at the moment. To continue our example, let's say that you choose the sixth statement as the one that rings most true.

In that case, change the sixth or top line of Hexagram thirty-five from solid to broken. This new hexagram is called the *Shih Kua* or "Evolving Hexagram."

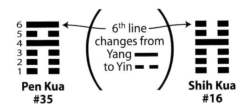

6
5
4
3
2
1

6th line changes from Yang ▬▬ to Yin ▬ ▬

Pen Kua
#35

Shih Kua
#16

Step 6) You now have two hexagrams that, taken together, represent your significant moment in the park. All that remains is for you to consult the appropriate chapters of the *I Ching* and follow the advice and instruction you find in each.

THE AUTHENTIC TAOIST WAY

Inner World Divination reveals the hidden energies involved at any given moment in spacetime. These energies are fundamental in providing us with a completely human experience of reality. As such, Inner World Divination is a gateway beyond the senses into the realm of the unknown that, once exposed, can be completely explored and navigated. Soon, totally new skills, thoughts, talents, and abilities can be called into experience.

The expertise necessary for calling these things into our field of reality is acquired by cultivating a lifestyle that is informed and guided by the Inner World method. Following the instructions and advice contained within the chapters reveals the intricate functions of consciousness and our energetic awareness of individual phenomenon in the natural world. It is then that we can fully align ourselves with the Tao and claim the wonders of the vast Universe as our own. This is the authentic Taoist Way.

THE STRUCTURE OF THE CHAPTERS

Each of the 64 chapters (or Canto, for the *Book of Changes* is a poem) of the *I Ching* presented in this volume contains the following information:

HEXAGRAM NUMBER: This is the traditional Canto numbering for the *I Ching*.

CHINESE NAME(S): These names are given in the two most popular methods for anglicizing Chinese: Wade-Giles and Pin-Yin. This will make it easier to reference contemporary *I Ching* scholarship, if you so desire.

ENGLISH 3-WORD NAME: The ancient Chinese name for each of the Cantos cannot sufficiently be expressed in one English word. Therefore, I use a system of Three-Word-Triangulation in order to clarify the true meaning. Don't think of these three words as choices of meaning. Rather, think of them as blending together to form a composite of meaning. Grasping the composite meaning opens the consciousness to subtle wisdom and flashes of intuition.

LINE ARRANGEMENT: The Canto itself is expressed in a combination of solid and broken 6-line graphs, i.e. the hexagram. Solid lines represent Yang energy at work, while broken lines represent Yin energy. Within the Taoist tradition the hexagram is a carefully constructed symbolic representation of the cosmic forces at play. In that capacity, it is a two-dimensional support for reflective meditation. Prolonged contemplation of any given hexagram will mystically reveal intuitive knowledge of the situation that it represents.

VERSE: This is an English translation of the secret *I Ching* verse from the Taoist oral tradition. These verses are compact enough to be easily memorized or recorded in a journal. Each of them is a condensed experience of *I Ching* wisdom that stretches back, literally, for millennia. Silently repeat the verse to yourself or recite it aloud. Contemplate the verse and allow it to stimulate your imagination, shape your intent, and suggest courses of thought and action.

MUSING WORDS: These are select words to be used for meditation and contemplation. They relate to the secret inner workings and constituent parts of the hexagram. More often, they form a record of mystic visions encountered by Taoist *I Ching* scholars of the past. Study these words carefully with regard to your question or situation. They contain clues of archetypal significance that relate specifically to you and your individual circumstances.

HIDDEN HEXAGRAM: This is the hexagram that lies at the heart of the main one presented in each chapter. It allows for a deeper penetration into the mysteries of the hexagram in question.

Every situation we encounter is composed of both obvious and underlying forces. It is these very forces and their related elements that the *I Ching* is designed to reveal. Once a situation is expressed in the form of a hexagram, the inner forces at work that lie at the heart of the situation can be thoroughly examined by consulting the wisdom of the Hidden Hexagram. This Hexagram is called the *Hu Kua*.

The Hidden Hexagram is composed of lines from the originally expressed hexagram. Specifically, the second, third, and fourth lines are used to form the bottom portion of the new hexagram, while the third, fourth, and fifth lines of the original hexagram are used to make the top portion. Studying the Hidden Hexagram will reveal the energies at work deep beneath the surface of any encounter.

MYSTIC WINDOW: This is advice given by a Taoist Master specific to aligning human behavior with the energetic dynamics represented by the hexagram. To put it simply, if you want to resonate harmoniously with the energy of the moment and produce the most positive outcome for yourself, then assiduously follow this advice. Think of it as your private window into the very heart of change.

ALCHEMIC WISDOM/ YAO TSI or LINE VERSE: These verses describe the specific kind of Qi exerting itself in your evolving situation. They also isolate the critical pivot point of change that is most strong and active at the time of consulting the oracle. The wisdom it provides is specific to you.

Critical Point of Change

In both consulting procedures (see pages 16 and 29), you made six statements and chose the one that resonated most with you in the moment. The number of the statement chosen determines the Line Verse that should be consulted for specific advice. (For example, statement number one coordinates with Line Verse number one. Statement number two coordinates with Line Verse number two, and so forth.) Closely follow the advice presented in the line verse. Remember, this is where the energy of change is most active for you. Since the line verse was chosen based entirely upon your own personal feelings, it reveals wisdom of a most intimate and profound nature. Because the line shows precisely where the energy of the situation is most active and changing, it also indicates specifically how the event will evolve and unfold.

The Shih or "Evolving" Moment

While the Yao Tsi reveals specific advice for aligning yourself with the single most active force of change in your situation, it also reveals the evolution of the situation—where your situation is going or what it's turning into. To determine the changing nature of your situation, simply change the most active line of your hexagram from Yang (solid line) to Yin (broken line), or Yin (broken line) to Yang (solid line).

For example, during the 3-coin consulting procedure, you constructed your hexagram from the bottom up. Therefore, if you decided that statement number two resonated most with you in the moment, change the line that is second from the bottom of the hexagram. If, on the other hand, statement number three rang most true for you, then change the line that is third from the bottom, and so on. It works the same way for the Inner World method, as well

Changing the chosen line to its opposite gives you an entirely new hexagram Taoists call *Shih* or "Evolved." This new hexagram will tell you precisely where your situation is heading. Consulting the wisdom of the Shih hexagram suggests ways for you to make the most of the changing situation before it occurs.

HEAVEN AND EARTH MEDITATION: Each hexagram of the *I Ching* is associated with one specific trigram. That trigram represents the fundamental shape of Qi at work deep within the hexagram. Once a hexagram is chosen, the cultivator attempts to shape the Qi of the bodymind and bring it in alignment with the Qi of the situation.

This uniquely Taoist meditation eventually ushers in cascades of transcendental wisdom. Indeed, this meditation represents an opening up to the forces of the Great Tao. Through an energetic conversation with the heavens and the earth, the Cultivator seeks to blend seamlessly with the primal forces at work within the heart of the situation. Simply put, it is an exchange of Qi energy between you and the Universe, designed to supremely clarify the moment. The top line represents the heavens and the bottom line represents the earth. The middle line represents mankind stretched between the powers of both.

Heaven and Earth Meditation is performed in a seated posture. Visualize life-force energy simultaneously moving either "into" or "out from" three different areas of the bodymind as graphically illustrated in each Canto. Each of these areas, called a *Tan Tien*, is a nexus of life-force energy or Qi. As the vital force of life, Qi moves objects and phenomena that exist in the natural world. It also moves through those objects and phenomena. This movement evokes a response in human beings that stimulates feelings and speaks to our individual nature.

The three Tan Tiens are referred to as the Upper, Middle, and Lower Heavens. Balance your contemplation of the hexagram name, verse, and musing words with the continuous exchange of energy taking place at each of these three bodymind areas. Doing so will generate higher states of awareness and allow you to penetrate the depths of any moment in spacetime.

MIND FOCUSING MEDITATION: This meditation is designed to hone and increase the mental powers of the *I Ching* Cultivator. When a hexagram is chosen, it directs you to a meditation specific to that moment, situation, or question.

Mind Focusing Meditation is accomplished by resting a portion of your awareness on a specific part of your physical anatomy while contemplating the hexagram. This inward focusing changes the Cultivator's inner landscape of Qi and alters the consciousness significantly. These areas become collecting points for the terrestrial energy that infuses the bodymind and elevates the intellect.

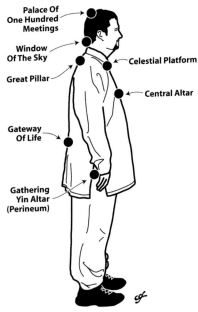

Strength Issuing Points

STRENGTH ISSUING MEDITATION: This meditation is designed to increase the overall physical strength of the *I Ching* Cultivator. While this meditation does engineer feelings of enhanced robustness, it does not generate brute force. Specifically, it augments the cultivator's motive force and vitality for living a dynamic and powerful life.

Taoist Strength Issuing is accomplished by imagining that the sum total of bodymind strength for living issues forth from one specific part of the anatomy. As the strength radiates outward from this point, it is envisioned as dramatically fortifying the workings of the entire bodymind. Strength issuing points are located on the front and back midline of the torso, head, and neck.

All three of these meditative techniques form the ancient foundation of Taoist Alchemy and Qigong (Life-Force Yoga). They may be practiced separately or together as you ponder the meaning of each hexagram. Taken as a whole, they are profound methods for generating health, wellness, and esoteric knowledge. Collectively, they represent a secret Taoist transmission presented here for the first time in any language.

Heaven/Begin/Initiate

Heaven above as below
Reflects itself with vitality and strength.
A perpetual sacrifice of polished jade
Begins the full moon's celebration.

MUSING WORDS:

Yang, Hand, Sun, Growing plants, Flying, Dragon, Life-force energy, Fire, Male

HIDDEN HEXAGRAM: # 1

MYSTIC WINDOW

Look for an opportunity to be creative, fun loving, and resourceful. Do not act withdrawn or introverted when dealing with people. Be aware of your life situation and gather information as needed. Look for inspiration where you find it.

Alchemic Wisdom
Yao Tsi (Line Verse):

1) The Dragon is hidden in the field;
   The Qi is insufficient for taking action.

2) The Dragon appears in the field;
   The Qi of questioning presents itself
   When consulting a Great Sage.

3) The gentle and wise man
   Remains devoutly creative all of his days
   But rests in relaxed awareness
   During the night.
   The Qi is fragile.

4) The Dragon lifts its head and prepares for
      flight.
   The Qi is expansive and burgeoning.

5) The Flying Dragon leaps to the heavens.
Sustain inquisitive Qi
When consulting a Great Sage.

6) No matter how high the Dragon flies,
It must eventually return to the earth.
The Qi moves up,
The Qi moves down.
Beware of the Arrogant Dragon.

Heaven and Earth Meditation:

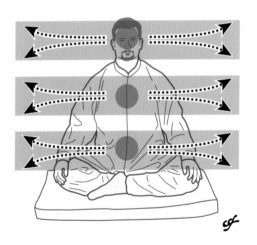

Mind Focusing Meditation:

Rest a portion of your mind in and around the small of your back and hold it there as you contemplate the meaning of the hexagram. Imagine that the Qi energy of your bodymind and the surrounding environment is condensing to that area, making you healthy and vibrant.

Strength Issuing Meditation:

Imagine that the force of your creativity, intuition, and physical and psychic strength radiates from the area known as the Ming Men or "Gateway of Life." (This energy Loci is located roughly between the second and third lumbar vertebrae.) Suggest to yourself that your entire organism is fortified by energy emanating from this area.

CANTO # 2 — K'UN/KUN

Earth/Receive/Respond

Earth above as below
Reflects itself by reaching out.
Immortal muses then appear
Supporting all that lives.

MUSING WORDS:

**Lightning, Rising smoke, Shrine, Incense,
Reverence, Soft, Female, Yin, Moon**

HIDDEN HEXAGRAM: #2

Look for an opportunity to express humility when dealing with others. Be authentic, spontaneous, and natural in all that you think, do, or say. Seek to be a follower instead of a leader and watch for the opportunity to rest in solitude.

Alchemic Wisdom
Yao Tsi (Line Verse):

1) The Qi expands;
The Qi condenses.
The earth opens up to receive
The energy of each and every step.
Winter approaches.

2) Be gracious of unfolding Qi
For it is organized and harmonious
And respectful of its own rules.
It has many uses.

3) Unfolding Qi stays hidden
From ordinary sight.
Likewise, be esoteric
In thought and action.
Unfolding has no end.

4) The Qi collects around itself.
It is discreet and innocent.

5) The Qi dives deeply into the ground.
Resonate with the Earth
And rest in its yellow center.

6) The Qi is beginning to change from within.
Dragons can be heard in the distance
Becoming restless and preparing for pitched battle;
Their blood twisting left and right
Seeking its core.

Heaven and Earth Meditation:

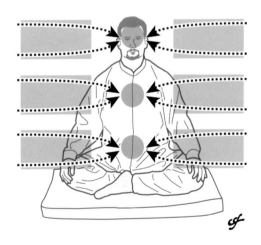

Mind Focusing Meditation:

Rest a portion of your mind on your hands and palms as you contemplate the meaning of this hexagram. Imagine them as collection points of earthly Qi. You may even fix your gaze upon them as a means of enlivening your spirit or Shen.

Strength Issuing Meditation:

Imagine that your strength for living issues from the Tien Tu or "Celestial Platform." This area is located in and around the notch in your throat. Imagine waves of refined strength radiating from this area and fortifying your entire bodymind. This force allows you to move through the natural world with strength and determination.

CANTO # 3 — CHUN/ZHUN

Sprout/Begin/Emerge

Rain clouds resting on thunder
Like a dragon's blanket
Define the boundaries of all things
Moved to growth.

MUSING WORDS:

**Clouds, Grass, Gather, Assemble, Ground,
Newborn, Seeds, Shallow water**

HIDDEN HEXAGRAM: #23

Alchemic Wisdom
Yao Tsi (Line Verse):

1) The Qi, initially blocked by a pillar of stone
  And sacred tree,
  Flows around the obstacles
  And seeks rest and guidance
  In the company of friends.

2) Moving forward
  Requires the momentum of
  Gathered strength and gathered Qi.
  Turn the horses, turn your hands in the clouds,
  Turn your very nature.

3) Qi moves in and out of the forest's heart.
  Do not enter without a guide and pathfinder.

4) Ride the wild forces of nature
As if you were in a soldier's procession.
Unite the Qi of individual gifts
And float on spacetime.

5) The Qi of emergence must remain small
Or the beginning will collapse of its own weight.

6) The spirit, force, and Qi
Of the natural world
Splits apart.
Disunity prevails.

Heaven and Earth Meditation:

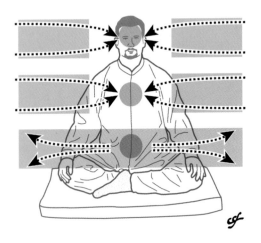

Mind Focusing Meditation:

Rest a portion of your mind on your spine as you contemplate the meaning of this hexagram. Alternately, you may focus on your entire back as the area of your bodymind where your Qi gathers. Imagine that your back becomes more defined and stable as the energy gathers there.

Strength Issuing Meditation:

Envision strength flowing from your Lower Tan Tien. This is an energy gathering spot located three and one-half inches below your navel and inward towards the physical center of your bodymind. The strength that flows from this area supports all that you think or do.

CANTO #4 — MENG/MENG

Conceal/Cover/New

A mountain stream seeks the valley
Where it lends itself
To cultivated land and soil
As a revealed force.

MUSING WORDS:

Hidden, Roof, Childlike, Wise, Enfold, Bushel basket, Twining grass (Dodder)

HIDDEN HEXAGRAM: #24

Look for opportunities to appreciate the points of view of others. Do not get lost in mindless activities and curb your desire to play too much. Stay relaxed, alert, flexible, and calm.

Alchemic Wisdom
Yao Tsi (Line Verse):

1) Quickly release youthful Qi.
Reach out to meet the moment
As if shackles bind your hands and feet.
Avail yourself of rules and order.

2) Protect youthful Qi
And receive the son's wife
By holding the gates open for her arrival.
Be willowy, yet weighted low.

3) Do not fully embrace the receptive Qi.
The metal man begins to move past you.
Make no plans;
Yield and overcome.

4) Stay alert to the Qi of the present ever
By embracing inner wisdom.

5) The Qi is innocent, childlike, and unspoiled.

6) Abruptly cease concealment.
Strike down the youthful Qi
With measured force.

Heaven and Earth Meditation:

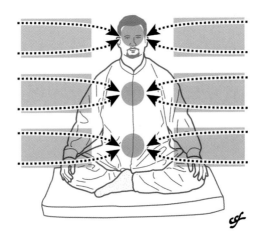

Mind Focusing Meditation:

Rest a portion of your mind on the palm of your open right hand. See this area as a point of focus for your will and life force energy. Remember, focusing on this area will help you discover the deep secrets of the hexagram.

Strength Issuing Meditation:

Your strength must radiate from the Palace of One Hundred Meetings, also known as the Pai Hui. This is the strength of the Tao Source of Life collecting at the crown of your head. Allow this strength to flow downward to every part of your bodymind as you contemplate the meaning of this hexagram.

CANTO #5 — HSU/XÜ

Patience/Rain/Waiting

Heavens hold the rain until needed
Waiting for the cloud's injunction
To release the dragon's tail
And move earthward.

MUSING WORDS:

**Drought, Prayer, Gather, Fortify, Halt,
Gravesite, Heaven's gate**

HIDDEN HEXAGRAM: #38

Look for a time to take stock of what you have and where you are going. We are all a collection of gifts and deficits and will act accordingly. Be aware of the difficulties that you encounter without succumbing to them. Be careful; danger is approaching.

Alchemic Wisdom
Yao Tsi (Line Verse):

1) Embrace the Qi of heart and patience.
Wait contently in the frontier.

2) Waiting by the fast moving river
Brings the confusion of whispered voices,
Amid strange and unrecognizable sounds.

3) Remain peaceful, calm, and relaxed.
Waiting in the mud steals your vitality.
Wading in the mud steals your mind.

4) Protect your blood and the middle heaven.
Stay within the Red Palace
And shun the pit of self-sacrifice.

5) The Central Palace
   Contains the distilled essence of mankind.
   Wait in the sacred space;
   The correct moment is about to be revealed.

6) Descend into the earth.
   Three unexpected wanderers will follow.
   Honor their descent
   With a sacrifice of spirit, vitality, and Qi.

Heaven and Earth Meditation:

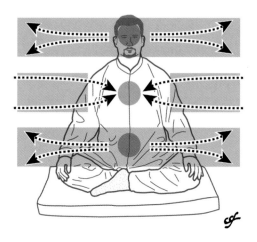

Mind Focusing Meditation:

Rest a portion of your mind on your breastbone as you contemplate the meaning of this hexagram. It's as if a hand is gently resting on this area as you study the *I Ching*. You can also focus on this area as you go about your day as a means of accessing the wisdom of the hexagram.

Strength Issuing Meditation:

The strength issuing point for this hexagram is the Upper Tan Tien. This is a spot located between the eyebrows, just above the nose and inward one inch from the surface of the skin. See waves of subtle strength radiating throughout your bodymind from this point. It is important that you are gentle with yourself during this meditation.

Contend/Dispute/Plead

There is opposition and argument
That calls for the caution
Of a soaring bird watching
A sleeping tiger.

MUSING WORDS:

**Punch, Earth, Speeches, Justice, Mountain's
base, Calmness, Prepare**

HIDDEN HEXAGRAM: #37

MYSTIC WINDOW

Be on the lookout for any confrontations or disputes that arise. When they occur, end them quickly and with great resolve. Yielding in the face of a greater force is the way of the Tao. Retreat rather than be overwhelmed.

Alchemic Wisdom
Yao Tsi (Line Verse):

1) Embody the Qi of new directions and new intent.
   Allow small words to be spoken and heard.
   But, pay them no mind.

2) You cannot sustain or support the conflict.
   Return home and nourish
   The three places.

3) Embrace the power and virtue of the Tao past.
   Learn from it and have no regrets.
   Ignore it and unending danger will follow.

4) Embrace Heaven's way of returning
   To the earth
   With simple order and peacefulness.

5) Let the conflicting Qi drop from your hand,
Returning it to the ground from which it sprang.

6) Accept the mystic belt that binds your life.
It will vanish when the three wanderers
Come forward.

Heaven and Earth Meditation:

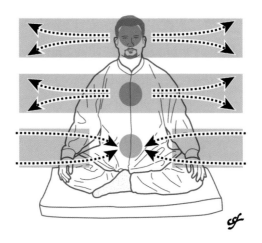

Mind Focusing Meditation:

Rest a portion of your mind on the back of your closed left fist. Suggest to yourself that a significant amount of your will, thought, and imagination is drawn to this area of your bodymind. Focus your mind and contemplate the hexagram.

Strength Issuing Meditation:

Feel strength radiating from the Gateway of Life and supporting your entire organism. The strength that comes from this area, which is also known as the Ming Men, clears your mind and allows you to deeply penetrate the mysteries of the sixth hexagram.

Multitude/Teacher/Society

Underground Streams and
Lines of force move deep
Beneath the feet
Of many Righteous people.

MUSING WORDS:

**Circular, Soldier, Citizen, Farmer, Reward,
Strategy, Respect**

HIDDEN HEXAGRAM: #24

MYSTIC WINDOW

Look for an opportunity to re-order those parts of your life that are important to you. Above all, be disciplined and organized at the start of any journey or endeavor. Be wary of inept leaders and govern yourself according to your higher ideals.

Alchemic Wisdom
Yao Tsi (Line Verse):

1) Gather your forces, muster your strengths, and Organize the Qi accordingly.
Disharmony obstructs virtuous expression.

2) Project yourself to the center of opposing forces And touch its native strength.
Three citations are issued by the ruler.

3) The army carries corpses to the wagons In preparation for retreating.

4) Retreating Qi is engaged;
Forces and strengths are preserved.

5) Lead the Qi and capture wild beasts that appear In the cultivated fields.

Bring the corners together with a centering
    action.
The oldest son takes the host captive and
    controls him;
The youngest minds the corpses that lay in the
    wagons.

6) The great prince issues simple commands,
Reorganizes the conquered lands,
Rewards his supporters and
Rests within the Qi of greatness.

Heaven and Earth Meditation:

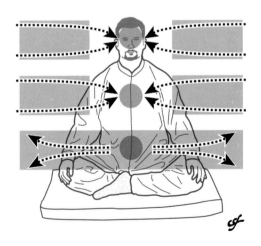

Mind Focusing Meditation:

Rest a portion of your mind on the fingertips of your open left hand while contemplating the deeper meanings of this hexagram. See each fingertip as a point of gathering Qi, blood, warmth, and relaxation. This will invigorate your entire organism.

Strength Issuing Meditation:

Issue strength from the area in and around your perineum. This area is known in Taoist cultivation as the *Hui Yin* or "Gathering Yin Altar." Imagine subtle strength flowing from this area opening up the arms and the legs. This engenders the ability to see things hidden from ordinary sight.

Singular/Union/Intimate

Northern stars do not rest
But rather are attentive and
Follow the smaller associations
Taking place upon the earth.

MUSING WORDS:

**Neighborhood, Cooperation, Five, Flood,
Ease, Repose**

HIDDEN HEXAGRAM: #23

MYSTIC WINDOW

Look for opportunities to build a consensus with those people close to you. Stand side by side with others to accomplish great things and look deep within yourself for confidence, strength, and inspiration. Be wary of ineffectual leaders even if that leader is yourself.

Alchemic Wisdom
Yao Tsi (Line Verse):

1) Harmonize the inner and outer worlds.
   Embrace the Qi of great meanings and
        substance.
   The expanded center of an earthen vessel
   Makes it useful.

2) Turn inward and protect your heartspirit.
   Be possessed of an inward loyalty and
   Unified actions will follow.

3) Doomsayers, fear mongers, and pessimists appear
   To steal your
   Qi (Life energy),
   Shen (Spirit or soul),
   Jing (Vitality),
   And loyalty.
   Shun them.

4) Exude loyalty and subtle strength outwardly.
Be intuitive and spontaneous.

5) A precise union of shape and function
Fills the heartspirit with kingly intent.
Three horsemen beat the brush,
Releasing wildfowl to fly forward.

6) Seek the Qi of leadership;
Exude strength like reeling silk.

Heaven and Earth Meditation:

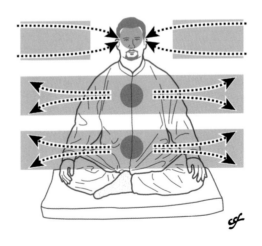

Mind Focusing Meditation:

Rest a portion of your mind on your open left palm. Imagine that your energies are gathering at this point while you are studying the hexagram. You may even imagine yourself holding the hexagram in your left hand.

Strength Issuing Meditation:

In order to grasp the secrets of the eighth hexagram, you must feel strength flowing from the area known as the Window of the Sky or Tien Ch'uang. As you go about your day contemplating this hexagram know that the strength for your inquiries comes from this area.

CANTO # 9 — HSIAO CH'U/XIAO XU

Accumulate/Small/Offering

Rising storms darken the skies
But no rain falls as yet
On the old man gathering
The strength of gold, swords, and jewels.

MUSING WORDS:

**Prepare, Storehouse, Truthfulness, Necessity,
Mysterious, Sincere**

HIDDEN HEXAGRAM: #38

MYSTIC WINDOW

Be on the lookout for complicated situations and remember that complex things are composed of simple things. Approach the complex with an eye towards this fact. Recognize where you are over-extended and pull back to rectify the situation.

Alchemic Wisdom
Yao Tsi (Line Verse):

1) Gather yourself
And return to the Tao Source of life.

2) Allow your Qi to be drawn out above and
below
Then return to the center place.

3) Thirty spokes around a hub make it useful.
The movement of a circle activates the wheel.
Protect the Shen (Spirit) as the cart moves
forward.

4) Manifest the Qi of conformity;
Invest in loss to shake the limbs,
Encouraging the buds to emerge as new
growth.

5) Harmonize the inner world with the outer world
And shape yourself to the moment.
Thus, you will bind yourself to great riches
Benefiting all those around you.

6) Rest and abide within the Qi of falling rain
As a place of nourishment.
Embrace the Tao Source of life;
Preserve the Yang and
Reproach no one.

Heaven and Earth Meditation:

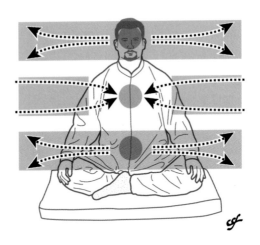

Mind Focusing Meditation:

As you contemplate the meaning of the ninth hexagram, rest a portion of your mind on your breastbone. Imagine a soft glowing light that gathers your thoughts and ideas like moths to a flame.

Strength Issuing Meditation:

To discover the secrets of this hexagram it is necessary to issue subtle strength from the area known as the Upper Tan Tien. This will fortify all of your inquiries. This point is a spot located between the eyebrows, just above the nose and inward one inch from the surface of the skin.

Action/Fulfill/Walking

Heaven walks upon the lakes
In steps of shade and shadow,
Telling us that firm action is taken
Best with light steps.

MUSING WORDS:

Upright, Duty, Deliberate, Forward, Shoes

HIDDEN HEXAGRAM: #37

Look for opportunities to approach situations with clarity and simplicity. Move naturally without hurry and without worry and be on the lookout for the best times to take action. Do not act impulsively.

Alchemic Wisdom
Yao Tsi (Line Verse):

1) Move forward simply
   With light and unadorned steps.

2) Move smoothly within the ever-turning Tao.
   Remain hidden, yet open to its wonders.

3) Be possessed of a warrior's Qi.
   Be vigilant even if half blind and half lame.
   Tread boldly on the Tiger's tail.
   Fight with resolve and solid purpose.

4) Remain very cautious when stepping on a tiger's
     tail
   And speak your mind for all to hear
   In a clear and elegant voice.

5) Resolutely move forward
And project a positive outcome.
Remain cautious and certain.

6) Take stock of the Qi generated
By your intent and your actions.
That which emanates from below
Must return from above
To a central place.

Heaven and Earth Meditation:

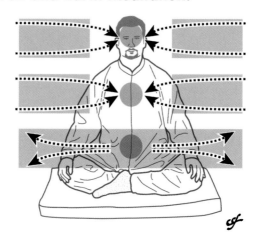

Mind Focusing Meditation:

Rest a portion of your mind on your breastbone while studying this hexagram. It will lift your spirits and aid you during your inquiries. This is especially true when combined with the Strength Issuing Point.

Strength Issuing Meditation:

Strength that issues forth from the Gateway of Life supports your entire organism as you work to unlock the secrets of the tenth hexagram. This energy center, located in the lumbar region, fortifies your thinking as well as your physical movements.

Great/Smooth/Advancing

Earth and heaven in prosperous union;
Moving, advancing steadily
While the full-flowered moon
Turns its head to emerge.

MUSING WORDS:

Wide, Sacred, City, Allow, Ritual, Steward, Mountain

HIDDEN HEXAGRAM: 54

MYSTIC WINDOW

Look for opportunities to be cooperative and helpful. This will probably entail stepping aside and letting things happen. Spend time with likeminded people who share your values and goals. A great leader is the servant of those he leads.

Alchemic Wisdom
Yao Tsi (Line Verse):

1) Pull out the weeds and overgrown grass.
Clear the field, turn the soil, and move forward.
Organize people
According to their gifts and deficits.

2) Embrace the wilderness.
Take responsibility for making it productive
And fruitful by infusing it with
Balance, poise, and equilibrium.

3) There can be no journey without a homecoming;
There can be no level ground without a
   mountain.
Qi moves out and moves in;
Qi rises and settles.
Join the heavens and the earth
With one hand above and one hand below.

4) Flying drunken immortal (Hsien)
Moving this way and that,
Alights where he finds food and drink.
What boldness!

5) Embrace optimism, exude subtle strength,
And radiate balanced Qi.

6) A great wall eventually sinks into the moat.
Consider the folly of persevering
In the face of disintegration.

Heaven and Earth Meditation:

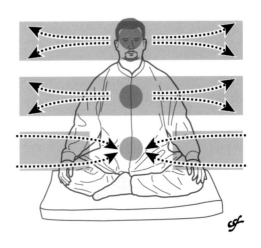

Mind Focusing Meditation:

Rest a portion of your mind on the back of a firmly closed right fist. This is your point of focus as you delve into the mysteries of the eleventh hexagram.

Strength Issuing Meditation:

The Gateway of Life is the area of your bodymind that supplies the strength to your entire being. See subtle strength radiating to every corner of your bodymind—in fact, each and every cell.

CANTO # 12 — P'I/BI

Stop/Halting/Close

The earth and sky
Cannot speak as they
Move away from each other
Acting like ambitious mirrors.

MUSING WORDS:

Mouth, Arrow, Open, Closing, Conserve, Bird

HIDDEN HEXAGRAM: #53

MYSTIC WINDOW

Look for opportunities to turn inward and listen
to your intuition. Remember that situations
mature in their own time. The laws of heaven
will not be rushed or impeded. Also, look for
opportunities to be alone as you work and
study.

Alchemic Wisdom
Yao Tsi (Line Verse):

1) Pull out the weeds and overgrown grass,
   Being careful not to make the hole too big.
   Clear the field, turn the soil, and move forward.
   Qi moves into the earth.
   Organize people
   According to their gifts and deficits.
   Solidly embrace the Qi of intuition.

2) Embrace common sense and
   Stand quietly by the plain and unadorned.
   Extend Qi to the simple man.

3) The offering is sacred.
   Honor the inner contract
   As well as the outer one.

4) Stretch up with the top of your head
And receive the power of the Heavens.
The community of souls seems divided
But acts with the Qi of unity.

5) Stop! Stand! Rest! Repose!
Dive into the earth seeking nourishment
And feel the thickness of life
Around you.

6) The Qi of change is the Qi of opposition.
Complete the sad hindrance
By turning it to joy.

Heaven and Earth Meditation:

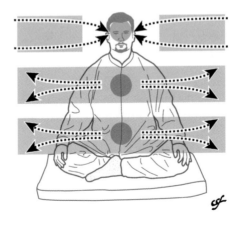

Mind Focusing Meditation:

Make a light fist with your right hand and rest a portion of your mind on the right fore-knuckle. Imagine that it is a lens that focuses all of the thoughts, feelings, and sensations that arise during your investigation into the twelfth hexagram. You may even focus your gaze on it as a means of clearing your mind and focusing your being.

Strength Issuing Meditation:

All of the strength for living that you possess comes from the Upper Tan Tien. This is a spot located between the eyebrows, just above the nose and inward one inch from the surface of the skin. See waves of subtle strength radiating throughout your bodymind from this point.

CANTO # 13 — T'UNG JEN/TONG REN

Similar/Harmony/Brotherhood

Fires touching the sky
Remind us that our paths
Are both the same and not the same.
Only the collected mind can be exposed.

MUSING WORDS:

**Lightning, Rising smoke, Shrine, Incense,
Reverence, Soft, Female, Yin, Moon**

HIDDEN HEXAGRAM: #44

MYSTIC WINDOW

Look for opportunities to engender trust in others and reaffirm your own moral sense. Do not work on your own. Be wary of unethical people and seek to avoid them. Associate with people of upright character that conduct themselves accordingly.

Alchemic Wisdom
Yao Tsi (Line Verse):

1) A gathering of men seek order
   Before entering the gate.
   Qi moves in freely
   And condenses to the bones of each
   Without any difficulty.

2) A gathering of men seek order
   Within a confined space.
   The Qi is not harmonious.

3) Contentious Qi gathers in the underbrush.
   It moves upward
   In groupings of three.
   There is no nourishment.

4) Seek high ground.
Qi moves Heavenward
Carrying you to safety.

5) A gathering of men begins with
Cries and wails.
It ends with fellowship and laughter.
The Great Host harmonizes the Qi
And creates success.

6) Go into the wilderness;
Seek the Qi of nature
And the harmony of the Tao.

Heaven and Earth Meditation:

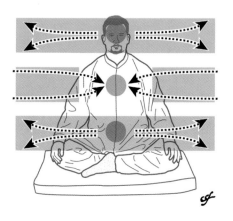

Mind Focusing Meditation:

Rest a portion of your mind on your spine and back. It's as if you are lying on your back with the ground beneath you. Feel your back and spine supporting you during your investigations into the meaning of the thirteenth hexagram.

Strength Issuing Meditation:

Issuing strength from the Lower Tan Tien will align your bodymind with the wisdom of this hexagram. Imagine that the strength and motive force needed for walking flows from this area. The Lower Tan Tien is located three and one-half inches below your navel and inward towards the physical center of your bodymind.

Great/Large/Harvest

Sun and fire as heat and light
Descend to the earth,
Subduing the darkness completely
As an illuminated mind begins to move.

MUSING WORDS:

Moon, Hands, Conceal, Giant, Possessions, Virtue

HIDDEN HEXAGRAM: #43

MYSTIC WINDOW

Look for the chance to expand your spirituality. Avoid pretentious and duplicitous behavior, especially if you are the source. Above all, act with clarity and simplicity after thoroughly examining any given situation.

Alchemic Wisdom
Yao Tsi (Line Verse):

1) A forced blending with unnatural Qi
Brings hardship and injury.
A forced blending with an unnatural mind
Brings confusion and error.
Claim safety and comfort as your own
And no problems will arise.

2) A big wagon used for transport
Carries people and things, both near and far.
You must have someplace to go
Before beginning your journey.

3) A man of great stature
And harmonious Qi
Can make a gift of himself
To Heaven.
A small man cannot.

4) Now is the time to issue strength.
   Qi expands;
   Qi condenses.

5) When all energies combine to make one,
   Each world can talk to the other.
   Qi, righteous and dignified,
   Shines out and dispels the darkness.

6) Heaven's power flows down from above
   And sanctifies the moment.
   Everything is blessed and correct.

Heaven and Earth Meditation:

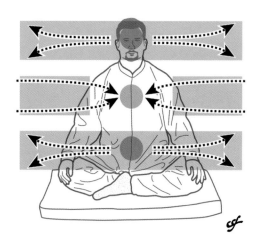

Mind Focusing Meditation:

Rest a portion of your mind upon your left hand closed into a fist. Raise your left fist to eye level and imagine that your energy and intent reside within it. This will help you decipher the deeper meanings of this hexagram.

Strength Issuing Meditation:

Your strength for delving into the mysteries of the fourteenth hexagram issues forth from that area on your bodymind known as the Gateway of Life. This strength supports not only all of your physical movements but your thought processes as well.

CANTO # 15 — CH'IEN/QIAN

Humble/Thorough/Modest

Mountains recede into the land by
Entering the earth and reducing itself
To forest and field
Where men and deer can feel its height.

MUSING WORDS:

**Mirror, Evenness, Dividing, Balance, Seek,
Benefactor**

HIDDEN HEXAGRAM: #40

MYSTIC WINDOW

Look for opportunities to remain still and quiet in meditation or thoughtful contemplation. Take advantage of any opportunity to grow and better yourself. Be wary of starting any project that you cannot finish and complete current projects by exercising self-control. Be disciplined, forthright, and modest in all things.

Alchemic Wisdom
Yao Tsi (Line Verse):

1) A superior man
   Humbly seeks the Qi of nourishment
   Beneath the surface.
   Self-conscious and reserved,
   He is able to safely cross the great stream
   And bring good fortune to all.

2) Become harmonious
   By becoming unassuming and humble.
   The oracle reveals simple Qi.
   Abide in this simplicity
   And good fortune follows.

3) Work slowly, measured, and modestly.
   Being unpretentious, the superior man
   Creates good fortune.

4) If you are unassuming and reserved
   The Qi of success and profit
   Cannot be far behind.

5) Abundance is denied.
   It is time to join with others
   And strike out
   In order to get what is needed.
   Embrace the Qi of modesty
   And even aggression will yield profit.

6) Make the sound of harmony
   And resonate with modesty and thoroughness.
   Gather the warriors and march forward.
   Subjugate the land of city and state.
   Consolidate your will and condense your Qi.

Heaven and Earth Meditation:

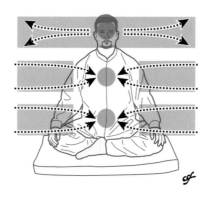

Mind Focusing Meditation:

Rest a portion of your mind on the center of your right fist. Envision all of your bodymind energies coalescing at this point. Taoist cultivators call this an Earth Centered Fist. Use it as a mental anchor as you contemplate the meaning of the fifteenth hexagram.

Strength Issuing Meditation:

In order to completely align your bodymind with the energies of change represented by this hexagram, strength must issue from the *Ming Men* or "Gateway of Life." Imagine that this strength provides you with the vitality necessary to conduct your investigations.

CANTO # 16 — YU/YU

Pleasure/Deep/Satisfaction

Thunder above the earth
Heralds the arrival of music
That must be seen, as heard,
With sprouts reaching for its source.

MUSING WORDS:

**Smooth, Graceful, Subdue, Tame, Elephant,
Help, Donate**

HIDDEN HEXAGRAM: #39

MYSTIC WINDOW

Look for opportunities to be optimistic and confident. Take the initiative in all affairs but do not boast or brag about past or future successes. Curb your current passions and identify with past experiences of personal significance.

Alchemic Wisdom
Yao Tsi (Line Verse):

1) Sounds that lift upward in delight
   Signal unfortunate occurrences.
   Qi that moves up
   Must move down eventually.

2) Embrace the Qi of solidity and firmness.
   Be as still as a rock.
   Without single-mindedness
   The moment cannot be concluded.
   The oracle calls for good fortune
   To those unswerving of energy and spirit.

3) Wide-eyed and astonished by pleasing spirits
   Brings sadness, regrets, and sorrow.
   Inaction in the presence of astonishment
   Multiplies sorrow.

4) Can you see the source of pleasure?
Gather subtle Qi at the crown of your head
And reveal the perennial source of great
   abundance.
Gather the like-minded amid the pleasure.

5) Remain stretched between
The Qi of Heaven and the Qi of Earth.
Stand firm and upright.
Even in sickness,
You will prevail.

6) Embrace the Qi of mysterious pleasures and
Moonless satisfaction that rises
From the depths of shadow.
Immediately make a change
And there will be no errors.

Heaven and Earth Meditation:

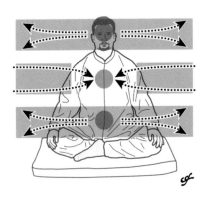

Mind Focusing Meditation:

Rest a portion of your mind on your breastbone while contemplating the meaning of this hexagram. See the energy, will, and imagination of your bodymind gathering in this area.

Strength Issuing Meditation:

In order to grasp the mysteries of the sixteenth hexagram, it is important to extend strength from the *Ta Chu* or "Great Pillar." This is particularly true as you go about your daily tasks while, simultaneously, contemplating the wisdom of the hexagram.

Connect/Lead/Follow

A Craftsman's hands proceed steadily,
Step by step
Uncovering the heart of thunder
That moves beneath the surface
Of the thing he makes.

MUSING WORDS:

Procession, Flags, Join, Footprints, Sword, Army, A General's power

HIDDEN HEXAGRAM: #53

Now is the time to adapt to conditions and follow the path of strength. Rise above your own ego and discard any pettiness you feel towards others. Now is definitely not the time to be small-minded. Align yourself with a higher goal and, accordingly, move resolutely forward. This is a perfect time for prayer and meditation.

Alchemic Wisdom
Yao Tsi (Line Verse):

1) Standing at the crossroads of change,
   Step through a gateway and ask for advice.
   Be firm, resolute, and unflinching
   As you wait for the song of change
   To rise from the earth.

2) Have regard for the Qi of the small,
   And you will lose the Qi of the great.
   This is a warning.

3) Have regard for the Qi of the great,
   And you will lose the Qi of the small.
   This, too, is a warning.
   Let the Qi lead.
   Let the mind follow and
   Abundance is assured.

4) Seizing abruptly brings misfortune.
Rest and abide within the Tao Source of life
And mystic illumination
Will surely follow.
Nothing can go wrong.

5) Rest and abide within the Qi of excellence
And abundance
Will surely follow.

6) The Qi is intertwined and connected to all.
It rests on the forest floor.
The ruler is engaged in offering sacrifices
To the land of awakening.

Heaven and Earth Meditation:

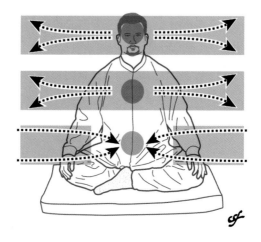

Mind Focusing Meditation:

Rest a portion of your mind on your wrists, fingertips, and backs of both hands. Cultivate a sense of lightness in these areas as you envision blood, warmth, and Qi flowing towards them. Taoist mystics regard these areas of your bodymind as holding the secret to fully understanding hexagram seventeen.

Strength Issuing Meditation:

During your studies of this hexagram imagine strength flowing from the Celestial Platform to all parts of your bodymind. This area is located in and around the notch in your throat. Remember, the strength that flows from this area fortifies everything you think or do.

Reduce/Distill/Destroy

Mountains contain invisible winds
Nourishing sleeping dragons not yet full
grown
While wizards above search for an antidote
To poison with poisons.

MUSING WORDS:

**Urn, Venom, Strength, Three, Potion,
Remedy, Worm**

HIDDEN HEXAGRAM: #54

MYSTIC WINDOW

Look for an opportunity to correct the mistakes of your forbearers. These could be blood ancestors or previous people who used to hold your position. Now is not the time to show weakness or hesitancy of any kind. Be direct, firm, and analytical as you work silently for the common good.

Alchemic Wisdom
Yao Tsi (Line Verse):

1) The father's business, fraught with confusion,
   Confronts the son with poisonous Qi.
   Clear the vision
   And no error will occur.
   Things now dangerous
   Will evolve to good fortune.

2) The mother's business, fraught with confusion,
   Presents poisonous Qi.
   It blocks the soul
   From making itself known.
   Seek the middle place.

3) The father's business, fraught with confusion,
   Presents poisonous Qi.
   The small-minded have much sadness
   But, there is no great error.
   Seek the lower place.

4) The father's poisonous Qi is condensed
And moves forward to a regrettable end.
Anchor yourself and gather vitality.

5) The father's poisonous Qi is transformed.
Uttering the sounds of passing
And great change,
Raises vitality.

6) A simple man's efforts
Transform the flawed work of kings and rulers
Into authentic expressions,
Which elevate and raise the spirit.
Stand alone.

Heaven and Earth Meditation:

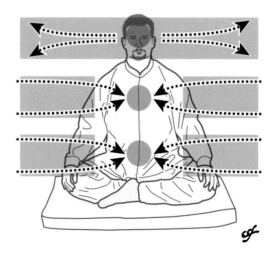

Mind Focusing Meditation:

Rest a portion of your mind in and around your shoulder joints. Imagine that the energy and intent gathering in each makes the whole bodymind very heavy. It's as if the weight of your shoulders tries to pull you into the ground.

Strength Issuing Meditation:

Imagine that strength is issuing from the Gateway of Life as you contemplate the meaning of the eighteenth hexagram. In combination with the Earth Focusing Meditation, issuing strength from this area will alter the consciousness of the entire bodymind. Thus altered, you will discover the secrets of Ku.

Draw/Approach/Nearby

Flying plateaus and generals,
Looking across a lake
Are watching tigers and waiting
For the moment to arrive.

MUSING WORDS:

**Lookout, Overview, Remote, View, Descend,
Wind, Lake**

HIDDEN HEXAGRAM: #24

MYSTIC WINDOW

Now is the time for you to act in a forward-looking manner. Be on the lookout for those who would get in your way and impede you. When you encounter individuals who behave like this, deal with it in a mature and relaxed way.

Alchemic Wisdom
Yao Tsi (Line Verse):

1) Everything comes together
   As the arrival of different kinds of Qi
   Heralds coming good fortune.

2) Everything comes together.
   The Qi of abundance and good fortune is
      forming.

3) Expansion begins as the Qi
   Moves together but separate.
   Abundance will not manifest
   Yet, harmony is maintained.

4) The single point of arrival
   Sits quietly at the center of expansive Qi.
   Harmony is maintained.

5) The soul speaks of wisdom and knowledge.
The harmonized man listens intently
For clues on how to move forward.
Good fortune abounds.

6) Authenticity presents itself.
The Qi of abundance
Insures success.

Heaven and Earth Meditation:

Mind Focusing Meditation:

Rest a portion of your mind on the palms of your upturned hands. Imagine that they want to float upward and away from each other. This will help you discover the inner workings of this hexagram.

Strength Issuing Meditation:

Imagine that strength is being issued from the Window of the Sky. After several minutes, shift your attention to the point of One Hundred Meetings. Maintain strength issuing from this point for several more minutes before returning concentration to the Window of the Sky. Continue alternating between the two. This will provide the alterations in consciousness necessary for a complete understanding of this hexagram.

CANTO # 20 — KUAN/GUAN

Observe/Reflect/Watch

Tigers looking from below
Feel the movement of the wind
By resting in the valley
And watching the moment unfold.

MUSING WORDS:

Eyes, Contemplate, Inward, Bind, Pour, Subdue

HIDDEN HEXAGRAM: #23

MYSTIC WINDOW

Now is the time for introspection and action that is based on thoughtful and careful planning. Look to your own self for clues on how to react. What factors are motivating you at this time? Knowing yourself will prevent mistakes. It is vital for you to be aware of any external circumstances that are overtly influencing your decision-making process. Do not stop thinking too soon.

Alchemic Wisdom
Yao Tsi (Line Verse):

1) A child sees what others cannot.
   Mystic wisdom is plain wisdom.
   Complicated reasoning brings great regrets.

2) Look quietly and simply
   Between obvious events
   And divine the authentic Qi.

3) What kind of Qi presents itself?
   Look to the life you surround yourself with.

4) Absorb the surrounding Qi.
Regard yourself as a visitor
In a strange land.
Be aware of the countryside.

5) Mindfully observe your own actions.
Look inwardly for clues
To outward events
And there will be no error.

6) Mindfully observe the actions of others
And see them as your own.
Go deeper into the moment.
Be centered, harmonized, and sure.
No errors will occur.

Heaven and Earth Meditation:

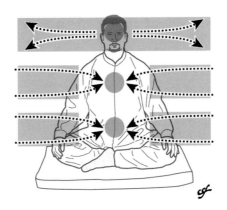

Mind Focusing Meditation:

Rest a portion of your mind on the opened palms of both hands. Imagine that the energy and willpower collecting in each causes them to be very heavy. In fact, if it were not for your effort, they would sink into the earth. Holding this idea in your consciousness will help you to unlock the secrets of this hexagram.

Strength Issuing Meditation:

Imagine strength issuing from the Tien Ch'uang or "Window of the Sky" located in and around the base of your skull. The image of subtle strength flowing from this area will support all of your intuitive investigations into the twentieth hexagram.

Bite/Remove/Erase

Heavenly fires meet earthly thunder
While plumes of incense rise
And breech obstacles
To sacrificial meat, bones, and metal.

MUSING WORDS:

**Close, Bring, Divination, Meeting Hall, Big
Dipper, Carefree, Noon, Happiness**

HIDDEN HEXAGRAM: #39

MYSTIC WINDOW

Look for the opportunity to correct small evils that come your way. Be on alert for larger evils and notify the proper authorities when they appear. Conduct yourself with undeterred resolution of thought and firmness of action.

Alchemic Wisdom
Yao Tsi (Line Verse):

1) The warrior's feet are imprisoned in stocks
And his toes are injured to the bone.
Mistakes are avoided and
There is no fault.

2) Bite through to the tender flesh
And cut off the nose
Of the offering.
No error if you turn inward.

3) Bite through the dried flesh and
Encounter thickness and old age.
Regrets are small happenings
Without error.

4) Bite into dried meat and bone
And reveal the refined substance
And riches of battle.

Stand upright and strong
With a warrior's Qi
And abundance will follow.

5) Bite through the dried flesh and
Encounter the refined substance
Of centered earth.
Be wary as dangerous Qi approaches.

6) He who is bound to the moment
Will wander lost and unnourished
In the upper world.
He can hear nothing
Of the approaching disaster.
Misfortune abounds from every quarter.

Heaven and Earth Meditation:

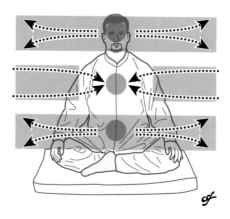

Mind Focusing Meditation:

Rest a portion of your mind on the closed fist of the right hand. If your mind becomes unfocused during your investigation of this hexagram, hold your right fist at eye level and focus your gaze upon it. Remember, this is a collection point for your will, thought, and imagination.

Strength Issuing Meditation:

Issue strength from the Gateway of Life to support cultivation of the twenty-first hexagram. Known as the Ming Men, this area is located in and around the Lumbar region of your spine.

Outline/Brighten/Elegance

Distant fires at the mountain's base
Outline the natural beauty
Of a like bird spreading its wings
To reveal its illuminated heart.

MUSING WORDS:

**Shell, Etiquette, Money, Flowers, Three,
Eternal, Decorate, Homage**

HIDDEN HEXAGRAM: #40

Look for an opportunity to rest and be at peace with yourself. Now is the time to romance your soul and cultivate your inner life. Harmonize your bodymind and indulge in simple pleasures.

Alchemic Wisdom
Yao Tsi (Line Verse):

1) Release the warrior's feet
   And decorate his toes.
   Put aside the carriages
   And set out on foot.
   Qi moves forward.

2) Decorate the warrior's beard.
   Qi moves upward.

3) The Qi adorns and moistens.
   Be firm and stand upright.
   Listen to your soul
   And abundance will follow.

4) Embrace the white Qi of the north
   And proceed as an unadorned bridegroom.
   Feel the Qi of a white winged horse
   Restrained at the cliff's edge.
   Come not as a thief but, rather, as a lover.

5) Embrace the Qi of humility
And present a gift of fine white cloth
In a lush and natural garden.
Seek the hills and raised places
And abundance will follow.

6) Embrace the simplicity
And white Qi of the north
And there will be no errors.

Heaven and Earth Meditation:

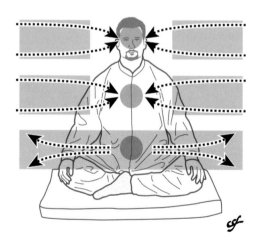

Mind Focusing Meditation:

Rest your attention on your breastbone and the little fingers of both hands. Imagine that your energy and vitality collects in these places. This will focus terrestrial energies inherent in your bodymind and help unlock the mysteries of the hexagram.

Strength Issuing Meditation:

Issue subtle strength from the area of your breastbone known as the Central Altar or *Chung Ting*. See this strength radiating outward and expanding your very being. This is an important clue to the hidden meanings contained in the twenty-second hexagram.

Carve/Erode/Scour

The ground beneath the mountain
Gradually decays and falls away
As the earth pulls back,
Stripping its heaven reaching power.

MUSING WORDS:

**Erode, Corrosion, Rusted sword, Sedate,
Regenerate, Home, Hopefulness, Assurance**

HIDDEN HEXAGRAM: #2

MYSTIC WINDOW

Be wary of competitors and traitors. Look for an opportunity to clarify your personal goals. Courageously set out to accomplish them in spite of the dangers. Now is the time to engage in seated meditation. Learn the fine art of keeping still.

Alchemic Wisdom
Yao Tsi (Line Verse):

1) Stripping the structure of its feet
Erodes its support and fundamental Qi.
The man has no mother.
Disregard your soul, remain unmoving,
And disaster will surely follow.

2) Cut it into pieces;
Reveal the Qi just beneath the surface.
Disregard your soul, remain unmoving,
And disaster will surely follow.

3) Cut it at the heart;
Reveal the Qi at its center
And study it closely.

4) Strip away the covering of the moment
And its sacred purpose will disappear.

5) Present a gift of strung fish to the court
And favorable Qi will abound
Among the beautiful women who gather there.

6) Behold!
A ripe fruit remains uneaten.
Surely, a great man gains much
By embracing the Qi of restraint.
The small men, however,
Tear at themselves for food.

Heaven and Earth Meditation:

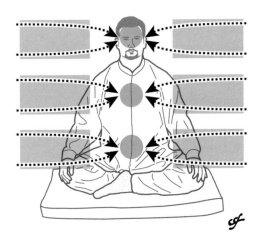

Mind Focusing Meditation:

Rest a portion of your mind on the palm of your opened right hand. Seeing this as a gathering point for the energy and force of your bodymind will usher you deeply into the esoteric meaning of the hexagram.

Strength Issuing Meditation:

Strength is issued from the place of One Hundred Meetings. When you begin to feel a light buoyant and sensitive energy gathering at your crown the blended forces of heaven and earth will intuitively reveal the wonders of the twenty-third hexagram to you.

Return/Revolve/Restore

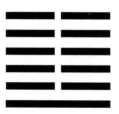

Thunderous rumbles beneath the ground
Signal the coming and going
Of an ancient force
That reveals the heart of the Tao.

MUSING WORDS:

**Seven (7), Footprints, Antiquity, Continuous,
Pull, Three (3), Tree**

HIDDEN HEXAGRAM: #2

MYSTIC WINDOW

Look for opportunities to exercise self-control
and strengthen your will. Avoid those who
would indulge your weaknesses and
obsessions. Above all, stand firm. Even in the
face of great opposition and jealousy, stand
firm.

Alchemic Wisdom
Yao Tsi (Line Verse):

1) Stop short and do not fill to the brim.
   Embrace the Qi of returning
   And have no regrets about turning back.
   Great abundance will follow.

2) The Qi of resolving and returning
   Reveals the abundant Tao Source of life.

3) Not rested, confused;
   Not knowing
   Whether you are coming or going.
   Incessant returning and second-guessing
   Is dangerous.
   Be cautious and wary and you won't misstep.

4) Walk the central path
Slowly and deliberately.
Walk alone and undisturbed
When turning back to the source.

5) Embrace the Qi of yielding and honesty.
Return to the source
And you will have no regrets.

6) Confusion abounds;
Evil multiplies one hundred times.
Reversal of fortune.
Move the army back home
Because the great defeat has already occurred.
The ruler will not recover for ten years.

Heaven and Earth Meditation:

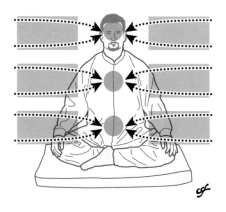

Mind Focusing Meditation:

Resting awareness on your breastbone will facilitate a gathering of terrestrial forces within your bodymind. When combined with the Strength Issuing meditation, this will reveal the energetic underpinnings of the twenty-fourth hexagram.

Strength Issuing Meditation:

Issue strength from the Gathering Yin Altar and you will be able to embrace the psychic core of this hexagram. Combining this with the above meditation will help reveal the complex inner workings of the situation it represents.

Authentic/Truthful/Sincere

Rolling thunder under the heavens
Signals the mindful approach of innocence
That walks steadily away from the expected
Towards the unexpected.

MUSING WORDS:

**Un-contrived, Archer, Natural, Innocent,
Correct, Honest, A jewel out of reach,
Spontaneous, Circumspection**

HIDDEN HEXAGRAM: #53

MYSTIC WINDOW

Look for opportunities to be patient and circumspect. Listen for wisdom coming from your intuition. Perform tasks for the sheer joy of doing them and avoid speculating about outcomes.

Alchemic Wisdom
Yao Tsi (Line Verse):

1) Embrace the Qi of honesty and authenticity.
   Resolutely set out on the path.
   Abundance abounds.

2) Do not worry about the outcome
   While doing the work.
   The fields are not plowed
   But they still yield a great harvest.
   Before you set out,
   Have a place to go.

3) A simple man is bound to oxen.
   Now he can rest and enjoy the journey.
   A complicated man fights the journey
   As the ox pulls him along.
   Embrace the Qi of surrender.

4) Listen to your heart and soul
And there will be no misstep.

5) Embrace the spirit of your illness
And you can heal yourself.
Be grateful within and without.

6) There is no place to go.
Even if you are honest,
There will be trouble.
Quietly stand firm.

Heaven and Earth Meditation:

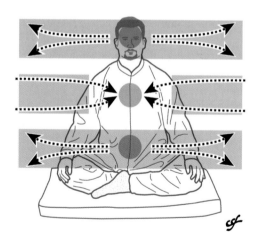

Mind Focusing Meditation:

Rest a portion of your mind on your back and spine. Envision these areas to be collection points of mental and physical energy. Maintain this focus as you intuitively investigate this hexagram.

Strength Issuing Meditation:

Issue strength from your Lower Tan Tien as you study the twenty-fifth canto. Envision subtle influence radiating from this area and fortifying your thoughts, words, and actions. This area is an energy gathering spot located three and one-half inches below your navel and inward towards the physical center of your bodymind.

CANTO # 26 — TA CH'U/DA XU

Offering/Exalted/Nourishment

Mountains reaching up will cradle the
Heavens
While a virtuous man,
Standing alone,
Engages consummate transcendence.

MUSING WORDS:

**Regal, Lofty, Noble, Freedom, Perseverance,
Moonlight, A test, Solitary dragon, Horses
unrestrained**

HIDDEN HEXAGRAM: #54

Be on guard for self-generated feelings of repression and insignificance. Look for opportunities to be charitable to others and allow the remarkable Tao to instruct you in correct and virtuous behavior. Avoid group-think or being swept away by the emotions of a crowd. Now is the time to embrace solitude.

Alchemic Wisdom
Yao Tsi (Line Verse):

1) Stop!
   Leave matters unfinished.
   Danger approaches from oblique quarters.

2) The Qi of support is broken
   And the axle has slipped away.
   It is impossible to continue.

3) A good horse will follow you
   Wherever you go.
   Practice the art of war:
   Movement, attack, defense.
   Embrace the Qi of the sun and the earth
   And have a place for rest and recuperation.

4) Move forward in a sacrifice of human energy.
Supreme abundance will follow.

5) Wear the talisman proudly.
Abundance will follow.

6) How does one speak to heaven?
Embrace the smooth Qi of the soul.
Reach up and heaven will reach down.
Enjoy unobstructed and continuous congress
With the Great Mystery.
Present yourself as an offering to the Tao.

Heaven and Earth Meditation:

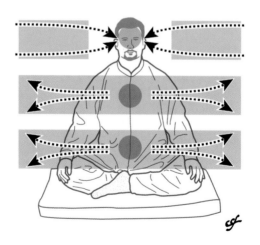

Mind Focusing Meditation:

Rest a portion of your mind on the palm of your opened right hand. See it as a gathering place for the terrestrial energies that give you life.

Strength Issuing Meditation:

Issue strength for the entire bodymind from the Tien Ch'uang or "Window of the Sky." This will support all of your investigations into the twenty-sixth Canto. This area is located in and around the base of your skull.

CANTO # 27 — I/YI

Nourish/Support/Nurture

Thunder splits the mountain,
Revealing the wisdom of
Nourishing the self by nourishing others.
Hidden dragons wait the call
Of creation.

MUSING WORDS:

**Prayer, Virtue, Rainfull, Three (3), Teeth,
Moderation, Crystalline**

HIDDEN HEXAGRAM: #2

Look for the opportunity to cooperate with your family, friends, and coworkers. Be of help to your superiors and reaffirm your connection to the Tao. Now is the time for solemn devotional activity.

Alchemic Wisdom
Yao Tsi (Line Verse):

1) Consult the oracle;
Speak with your soul.
Ignore the dictates and disaster follows.

2) Stop!
Do not proceed.
The force of life assails you.
There will be catastrophe if you move forward.

3) Shake off the assault and
Consult the oracle.
The Qi of catastrophe is still present
And will be for some time.
There is no place to go
To find abundance.

4) The assault grabs your attention
And rouses your spirit to action.
Abundance is here for the taking
If you are tenacious in your pursuit.

5) The tree is shaking;
The horse is trembling.
Listen to your soul and follow its dictates
But do not cross the great stream.
Sufficient abundance is already present.

6) Seek nourishing Qi and
Steel yourself to the Danger.
The abundance is yours if
You cross the great stream.

Heaven and Earth Meditation:

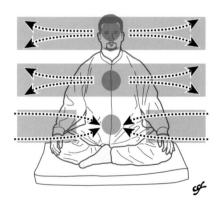

Mind Focusing Meditation:

Focus the terrestrial energies of your bodymind by resting a portion of your mind on your closed right fist. Squeeze gently but firmly as you envision a condensation of will, energy, and vitality taking place in this area.

Strength Issuing Meditation:

In order to plumb the depths of wisdom in this canto, you must imagine strength radiating from your Lower Tan Tien. This subtle strength provides the motive force of your investigations into this hexagram. The lower Tan Tien is an energy gathering loci located three and one-half inches below your navel and inward towards the physical center of your bodymind.

CANTO # 28 — TA KUO/DA GUO

Exalter/Ordinary/Beyond

The lake's power surpasses the winds,
Warning of sagging roofs
And flowers on a dead tree
Yielding to an accumulation of great burdens.

MUSING WORDS:

Passage, Threshold, Red, Doorway, Extraordinary, Excess, Entreat, Chariot, Small box

HIDDEN HEXAGRAM: #1

Now is not the time to be impetuous or foolhardy. Be mindful of careless behavior, especially when pursuing worthwhile goals. Look for a new way to express your talents and watch for uncommon inspiration coming from common quarters.

Alchemic Wisdom
Yao Tsi (Line Verse):

1) Prepare a sacred space and honored precinct
   Of simple, yet powerful, means and
   Surrender to the forces of Heaven and Earth.

2) New growth
   Appears after a judicious pruning.
   Settle down to a simple way of life
   And the life of your way will be blessed.

3) The center of the roof has become misshapen.
   It weakens the entire building.
   It threatens all who live beneath it.
   The Qi of misfortune abounds.

4) The center of the roof is straight and strong.
Abundance lives beneath it.
If it begins to sag,
You will have many anxious moments.

5) New growth springs forth
From an unexpected place.
Be pleased but not arrogant or boastful.

6) Look beyond your obvious gifts and deficits.
Be adventurous
And dare to embrace the Qi of advancement.

Heaven and Earth Meditation:

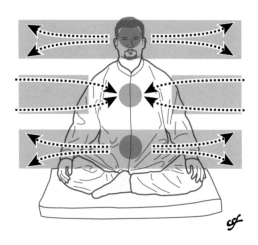

Mind Focusing Meditation:

Rest a portion of your mind on the back of your closed left hand. The back of your left fist contains a secret clue to deciphering the hidden meaning of this hexagram.

Strength Issuing Meditation:

The Window of the Sky is the seat of strength that supports a bodymind investigating the twenty-eighth canto. In Taoist parlance, the esoteric wisdom gleaned from this meditation, "rests upon the shoulders and warms the back of the cultivator."

CANTO # 29 — K'AN/KAN

Plunge/Blackness/Pit

The double darkness of a gloomy rain
Conceals the need to flow from the heartmind
Amid the turning of the great wheel
Unfettered by dangers and pit falls.

MUSING WORDS:

**Danger, Intense, Snakes, Confinement,
Waterfall, Entrapment, One hand and foot,
Abyss**

HIDDEN HEXAGRAM: #27

MYSTIC WINDOW

Be on the watch for confused thinking in yourself, as well as others. Seek to flow around obstacles as if you were water seeking a place of rest. Now is the time to avoid complicated and nuanced thinking. "Clarity" should be your watchword.

Alchemic Wisdom
Yao Tsi (Line Verse):

1) The pit is deep and foreboding.
   To enter it is to enter an evil place.

2) The pit is very dangerous.
   Seeking solace and advice from your soul
   Is useless.

3) The pit is all around you
   And you are bound to the dangerous Qi.
   It does no good to confront the evil.

4) There is a way out of this evil place.
   Sacrifice earthly energies
   With both hands.
   Embrace the Qi of illumination
   And you will save yourself.

5) Your perspective must change.
See the pit in a new light
And you will glimpse a way out of it.

6) The only way out is fraught with danger.
You will have to be patient for some years.
Misfortune gathers around you in groups of
three.

Heaven and Earth Meditation:

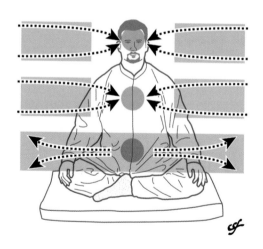

Mind Focusing Meditation:

Envision energy, vitality, and willpower collecting at the finger tips of your right hand. It's as if you have dipped them into warm liquid that has, somehow, facilitated the gathering. When this focusing is used in conjunction with the following strength issuing meditation, "the five elements combine to reveal the secret of the hexagram."

Strength Issuing Meditation:

The cultivator of this hexagram should see continuous waves of strength radiating from the Gathering Yin Altar located in and around the perineum. This will support a deep investigation into the secrets of the Canto.

Fire/Light/Sun

The double rising of the sun and moon
Reveals a force flowing from the center
That meets brightness with brightness
And leaves dark times behind.

MUSING WORDS:

**Wisdom, Intellect, Elegant, Ghostly, Birds,
Flames, Wings**

HIDDEN HEXAGRAM: #28

Look for the opportunity to be clear and direct, yet not pedantic or overpowering. A bright light can cast deep shadows and engender great fear in others. Soften your light but remain enduring. Cultivate optimism and a positive mental outlook on life.

Alchemic Wisdom
Yao Tsi (Line Verse):

1) Walk slowly, deliberately, and reverently.
   You will not misstep.

2) Radiant colors of gold and yellow
   Dancing from the fire
   Ensures great abundance.

3) The sun moves resolutely across the sky
   And sets
   Carrying the radiant Qi with it.
   This is the natural way;
   So it is with life.
   An aged man approaches his own sunset.
   Do not reminisce about the past.
   Enjoy the approaching twilight.

4) The flames suddenly flare brightly
And, just as suddenly, die down.
The coming Qi is likened to a burning.

5) Mourn and remember what has passed.
Proudly carry your loss.
Sigh and moan.
Abundance will appear.

6) War is sometimes necessary.
The king uses it wisely.
He knows that death is a part of life.

Heaven and Earth Meditation:

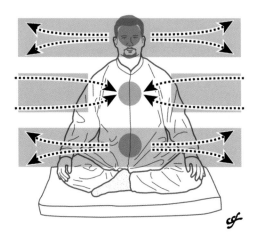

Mind Focusing Meditation:

Rest a portion of your awareness upon your Upper Tan Tien area. In conjunction with the heaven meditation, this will set the stage for an intuitive investigation into the thirtieth Canto. This area is a spot located between the eyebrows, just above the nose, and inward one inch from the surface of the skin.

Strength Issuing Meditation:

Issue strength from your Lower Tan Tien area as you explore this hexagram. This will boost your intuition and grant you the ability to "see the soul of Li" as an energy gathering spot located three and one-half inches below your navel and inward towards the physical center of your bodymind.

CANTO # 31 — HSIEN/XIAN

Outreach/Stimulate/Influence

Scholars and poets
Gather at mountain lakes
To speak words of making
That uplifts the heartmind of humanity.

MUSING WORDS:

**Compel, Together, Poesis, Move, Conjunction,
Alignment, Sincerity, Song**

HIDDEN HEXAGRAM: #44

MYSTIC WINDOW

Now is the time to listen carefully to precisely how others employ words. Remember, words mean things. So be careful how you use them. Think before you speak. Avoid situations over which you have no control. Look for opportunities to be circumspect.

Alchemic Wisdom
Yao Tsi (Line Verse):

1) Movement at the end
Of the leg;
The big toe points forward.

2) Movement at the middle
Of the leg;
The calves twitch.
To stay rooted brings abundance
But there is sorrow in moving
Forward.

3) Movement at the top
Of the leg;
The thighs flex and prepare.
Hold your position and Qi will follow.
Going forward brings disappointment.

4) Consulting the oracle reverently
   Brings abundance and absence of worry.
   Indecision is contagious.
   Do not hesitate
   Or you will reveal your private self.

5) Movement in your back and spine.
   Lift the back and raise the Qi,
   And you will have no regrets.

6) Movement in the mouth.
   The teeth are lightly clenched
   And the tongue revolves within.
   Sweet dew descends to the Lower Heaven.

Heaven and Earth Meditation:

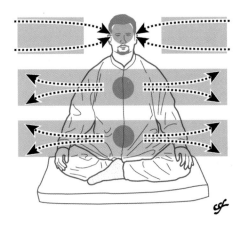

Mind Focusing Meditation:

Rest a portion of your mind on the palm of your right hand. Here the earth energies present within your bodymind gather to support your intuitive investigations of hexagram thirty-one.

Strength Issuing Meditation:

Issue strength from the Gateway of Life. See strength flowing from this area that motivates all of your bodymind movement. This will help put you in touch with the secret wisdom contained in this canto.

Natural/Heartmind/Constant

As thunder and wind are joined,
So are the sun and moon joined
In a perpetual dance
And reflective life-long journey.

MUSING WORDS:

**Clearing, Doorway, Two (2), Middle, Boats,
To listen, To talk**

HIDDEN HEXAGRAM: #43

MYSTIC WINDOW

Look for the opportunity to expand the breadth
of your activity and not the depth. Focusing on
one thing will bring confusion. Specialization is
not the useful way for you to realize the best of
the present situation. Do not be hasty or
indecisive. Instead, wait for the precise moment
to be enduring.

Alchemic Wisdom
Yao Tsi (Line Verse):

1) Repeated digging accomplishes nothing.
   The Qi is without purpose
   And abundance is nowhere to be found.

2) Embrace the Qi of openness
   And regrets will disappear.

3) His morality is convenient and changeable.
   This is disgraceful.
   The soul entreats forgiveness for the penitent.

4) No life can be found
   Within the ground of being.
   The field is devoid of game.

5) His morality is fixed, constant, and fair.
This is laudable.
Intuition brings abundance;
Reasoning brings misfortune.

6) Neither focused nor orderly
Shaky behavior brings calamity.
The Qi wanders and is confused.

Heaven and Earth Meditation:

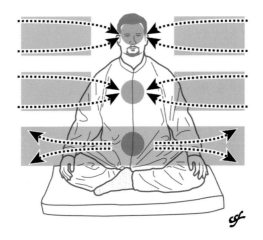

Mind Focusing Meditation:

Rest a portion of your mind on the palm of your left hand and envision the earthly energies within your bodymind collecting and condensing there. Ancient Taoist wisdom holds that the secret to deciphering this hexagram lay within the palm of the left hand.

Strength Issuing Meditation:

Your investigations of this canto must be driven by waves of strength emanating from the Central Altar. Remember, this strength, issuing from the area in and around your breastbone, is very subtle and expansive in nature.

Withdraw/Secluded/Stop

A mountain under the heavens
Is an iron fortress of solitude.
With gathered strength and protected
essence,
Secure the heart of illumination.

MUSING WORDS:

**Footprints, To track, Stalk, Small animal,
Single-handed, Retreat, Sacrifice, Offering**

HIDDEN HEXAGRAM: #44

MYSTIC WINDOW

Now is the time to be patient and calm.
Mindfully observe all that is occurring around
you and carefully gather all of your resources
and thoughts. Do not become self-indulgent or
weak in the face of opposition or tragedy.
Instead show courage and resoluteness. Now
is not the time to play the victim.

Alchemic Wisdom
Yao Tsi (Line Verse):

1) A hidden tiger tail signals danger.
   Keep still and attract no attention.

2) Assume a disguise
   And conceal your authentic self.
   Drop the charade at your peril.

3) Convictions bind you to yourself
   And imprison you at the same time.
   Diseased and dangerous Qi abounds.
   Indulge yourself and enjoy what you already
        have
   For abundance begets abundance.

4) Conceal your good nature and compassion
And you will be elevated.
Abundance abounds.
An ordinary man will not heed this warning.

5) Conceal your excellent virtue.
Listen as your soul speaks
And abundance will manifest swiftly.

6) Hide your wealth.
Conceal your riches
And you will gain a supreme advantage.

Heaven and Earth Meditation:

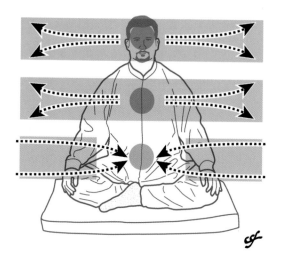

Mind Focusing Meditation:

Focus your earthly energies in your lower back as you investigate the deeper meanings of this Kua. Remember, this is an area of collection, order, and consolidation. Gently rest a portion of your mind there.

Strength Issuing Meditation:

Issue strength from the Gathering Yin Altar. This will support your study of the canto. The Gathering Yin Altar is also known as the Hui Yin and is located in and around the perineum.

CANTO # 34 — TA CHUANG/DA ZHUANG

Great/Unwise/Strength

The sound of thunder above heaven
Signals a warning when using great strength;
Employ power and force judiciously
As if wielding an ancient weapon.

MUSING WORDS:

**Robust, Big, Overburdened, Force, Power,
Uninformed, Collapse, Big Dipper, Pole star,
Ram butting**

HIDDEN HEXAGRAM: #43

MYSTIC WINDOW

Be very cautious when using power or strength
of any kind. Wise force isn't rash or undirected.
It is specific rather than wasteful. Attempt to
see the big picture and make specific plans
based upon this overview. Avoid all pettiness
and obsession.

Alchemic Wisdom
Yao Tsi (Line Verse):

1) Strength at the end
   Of your leg.
   Hold it back and do not walk forward
   Or disaster will befall you.

2) Embrace intuitive Qi
   And abundance follows.

3) The brash man uses brute force
   And direct action.
   The superior man employs the subtle strength
   Of non-action.
   The brash man, imprisoned by his actions,
   Defeats himself.

4) With a wave of the hand
The Qi of imprisonment is brushed away
And all sorrows vanish.
Embrace the Qi of a great wheel
With thirty spokes.

5) Change directions and lose a few of the flock.
There is no cause for blame
As change invariably brings necessary losses.

6) You cannot move forward;
You cannot move backward.
A single-minded ram pushes against a wall
To no avail.
No position is good.
Wait and difficulties will change to abundance.

Heaven and Earth Meditation:

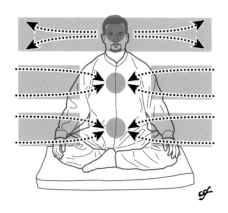

Mind Focusing Meditation:

Rest a portion of your mind on your left palm. You may imagine that you are holding the Musing words with it. Gently focus your mind on this area.

Strength Issuing Meditation:

Your investigations into the deeper meanings of this hexagram should be supported with strength issuing from that area known as the Window of the Sky. Also known as Tien Ch'uang, the Window of the Sky is located in and around the base of your skull.

Progress/Advance/Flourish

Campfires on the distant horizon
Signal sunrise and nightfall
While two swallows flick their tails and
Fly steadily towards the sun's heart.

MUSING WORDS:

**Sunrise, Breeze, Inner, Outer, Abdomen,
Cauldron, Horizon, Spring growth, Increase**

HIDDEN HEXAGRAM: #39

MYSTIC WINDOW

Seize the moment but make haste slowly. Now is not the time to go it alone. Seeking a partnership is very advantageous if both parties are certain that they share the same goals. Wait for the occurrence of a happy accident, and then deliberately move forward. Do not embark on a self-improvement regimen at this time.

Alchemic Wisdom
Yao Tsi (Line Verse):

1) To show something off
   Is to destroy its essence.
   Being circumspect and reserved
   Erases error and brings abundance.
   Project your soul
   With poise and self-assurance.

2) To show something off
   Is to make it a sorrowful thing.
   Your soul instructs you
   To don a warrior's coat
   And pay homage to your family.

3) Everything is centered.
All guilt fades away.

4) To show yourself off
Brings calamity and great danger.

5) Sorrow and guilt have all but faded
And you take a relaxed view of things.
Proceed slowly without apprehension
And abundance will unfold before you.

6) A frontal attack is used to punish the city.
There is great danger that hides abundance.
And, while no mistakes are made,
You will still be full of remorse.

Heaven and Earth Meditation:

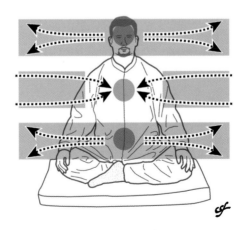

Mind Focusing Meditation:

Rest a portion of your mind on both the palms and backs of your hands. Imagine that, as the energies gather, they become as light as feathers.

Strength Issuing Meditation:

Strength must be issued from the Central Altar if you are to be successful in deciphering the deeper meaning of this hexagram. The Central Altar, also known as Chung Ting, is located in and around the area of the breastbone.

Bright/Illumination/Injured

Fire plunging beneath the earth's surface
Finds fire center and bides the fire time.
A shining bird flying from the setting sun
Forms the image of
A bodymind enveloped by sun and
moon brilliance.

MUSING WORDS:

**Wounded man, Risk, Intelligence,
Understanding, Bow and arrow, Barbarian**

HIDDEN HEXAGRAM: #40

Gather your strength and collect your life-force energy deep within. Seek inner nourishment. Now is a good time for meditation and personal cultivation. Listen to your heart and it will reveal the weaknesses of any person or situation that approaches you. It is vitally important that, at this time, you keep your plans to yourself.

Alchemic Wisdom
Yao Tsi (Line Verse):

1) Birds in flight vigorously
   Reveal the Dragon's tail.
   The brightest bird leaves the flock,
   Stretches its wings, and floats alone.
   The elevated man fasts and walks for three days
   Then, stops.
   There is a place to go.

2) The brightest bird is wounded.
   It cannot rely upon the intuition for support.
   Seek help from a strong horse
   And abundance will abound.

3) The brightest bird turns south
And goes hunting.
The great hunter should accompany you.
Do not interpret the soul's dictates
Too quickly.
Be very mindful.

4) Enter the belly of the brightest bird,
Seize the heart of the moment
And hold it up for all to see.

5) Consult the oracle and make an offering
To the spirits of the past.
The brightest bird's heart shines out
Even when hidden behind a cloud.

6) Brightness is gone and only darkness remains.
Honor the moment by
Stretching upwards to receive heaven
Then, extend downward into the earth.

Heaven and Earth Meditation:

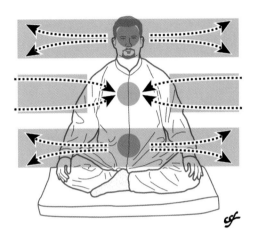

Mind Focusing Meditation:

Collect a light, buoyant, and sensitive energy at the crown of your head. Imagine that it gently pulls you upward toward the heavens.

Strength Issuing Meditation:

Issue strength from that area known as the Central Altar. Use this strength to support your intuitive investigations into the esoteric meaning of the thirty-sixth hexagram.

CANTO # 37 — CHIA JEN/JIA REN

Family/Deportment/Relationship

Hot winds rising from the hearth,
Bring order and comfort to the family.
When each family member honors their role,
Their strengths fuse and they become
indomitable.

MUSING WORDS:

**Archer, Ancient texts, Clouds, Genuflecting,
House, Beautiful woman, Happiness,
Mankind**

HIDDEN HEXAGRAM: #64

MYSTIC WINDOW

Now is the time to embrace simplicity of action
and clarity of mind. Write down your goals
and honor your desire to accomplish them. It is
not the time to strike out and forcefully move
forward. Be gracious in leadership, gentle in
correcting others, and patient when listening to
others. Above all, be gentle and optimistic with
yourself.

Alchemic Wisdom
Yao Tsi (Line Verse):

1) Establish limits and boundaries
   With your neighbors
   And all disappointments will vanish.

2) Stay close to home
   And focus on nourishing your family.
   Your soul reveals abundance.

3) The family is unruly and needs discipline.
   Self-imposed limits bring abundance.
   Ignoring the undisciplined family
   Brings sorrow and remorse.

4) The Qi of abundance abounds.
Great wealth flows through the family.

5) Join with your kith and kin.
Seek harmony and congress in your own house
And there will be no worry.
The Qi of nourishing abundance
Rises from the earth.

6) Strength and virtue issue from
A self-confident and self-assured place.
Proceed with a calm regalness
From a stable home
And abundance will present itself.

Heaven and Earth Meditation:

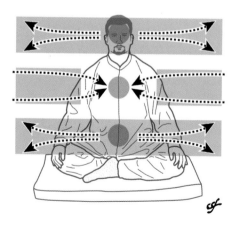

Mind Focusing Meditation:

Rest a portion of your mind on your closed right fist. Gather and collect your Qi to this area to support your investigations into the thirty-seventh hexagram.

Strength Issuing Meditation:

The Gateway of Life or Ming Men supplies all of the inner strength necessary to decipher the message of this hexagram. This area is located in and around the lumbar region of the spine.

Contend/Strange/Grapple

A burning lake blocks the way.
There is no room to move through possibilities
Because eyes are blinded by closeness.
Two women cannot run one household.

MUSING WORDS:

**Diverse, Closed gates, Small victories,
Trapped tiger, Heavy axe, Renewal, Peach
blossoms, Winter goose**

HIDDEN HEXAGRAM: #63

MYSTIC WINDOW

Investing in loss will yield small gains and personal satisfaction. Seek peace amid confusion and relinquish control as a means of overcoming adversity. Yield to overcome; bend to be straight; have little and gain much; empty and be full. Seek a cooperative ally and value the help he provides.

Alchemic Wisdom
Yao Tsi (Line Verse):

1) Be on guard
   And listen with your heartmind
   For evil men are everywhere.
   Mindfully embrace the action of non-action
   And that which is lost
   Will, naturally, be found.
   Do not force the issue
   And mistakes will not occur.

2) Seek out a teacher of the Tao Way of life
   And meet him halfway.
   He will show you how to avoid blunders.

3) The wagon is bogged down.
The team of oxen is exhausted.
The leader is directionless
And cannot hear the dictates of heaven.
Cut off from the Tao Source,
Things are not off to a good start.

4) Let the spirits guide you
And you won't misstep.
But, be very careful.
Ghosts often speak in riddles.

5) The time is now!
The vision is cleared!
Seize the moment and move forward quickly.
How can you fail?

6) A play of quizzical ghosts
Displaying conflicting mysteries.
Bound and unbound;
Gathered and released;
Coming and going.
Embrace the Qi of non-action
And the riddle is solved.

Heaven and Earth Meditation:

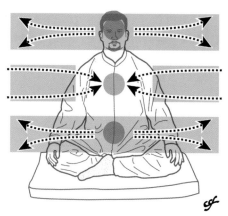

Mind Focusing Meditation:

Gently rest a portion of your mind on Lower Tan Tien as you intuitively investigate the mysteries of this hexagram. This area is an energy gathering spot located three and one-half inches below your navel and inward towards the physical center of your bodymind.

Strength Issuing Meditation:

Issue strength from the lumbar area known as the Gateway of Life as you search the canto for the hidden meaning of the thirty-eighth hexagram.

CANTO # 39 —
CHIEN/JIAN

Falter/Difficulty/Personal Burden

Water is resting frozen on mountaintops.
Elemental drums signal a moving towards darkness.
The cold stare of something distant and unseen,
Abruptly alerts you to its presence.
Stand firm.

MUSING WORDS:

Lame, Limping, Sudden danger, Intuition, Consolidate, Compassion, Happiness, Deliberate, Surprise

HIDDEN HEXAGRAM: #64

MYSTIC WINDOW

Be alert and mindful in everything that you do. At this time, any action that is both slow and measured, and that follows a simple plan, is the most favorable kind of action. Stay close to home and family. Selflessly give them whatever assistance they require. Now is a good time to learn a new skill and receive instruction from a teacher or mentor.

Alchemic Wisdom
Yao Tsi (Line Verse):

1) Setting forth and pressing forward
   Causes problems.
   Arriving naturally, unhurried and unworried,
   Brings praise.

2) Outward difficulty
   Is linked to
   Inward difficulty.
   You are the cause of the problem.
   Resolve, first, your own heartmind.

3) Problems block your path.
   Return to the Tao Source
   And the Tao Way will be clear.

4) Problems block your path.
Seek help from the like-minded.
The Qi of forward motion relaxes.

5) Great difficulty presents itself,
But do not despair.
True friends and companions will appear
And provide the help you need.
Embrace the Qi of hopefulness.

6) Setting forth and pushing forward
Causes problems.
Arriving naturally, unhurried and unworried,
Brings abundant Qi.
Seek out an elevated and wise man.

Heaven and Earth Meditation:

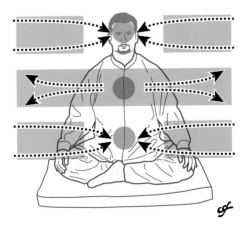

Mind Focusing Meditation:

Rest a portion of your awareness on your back and spine. See earthly energies gathering there and employ it as a means of focusing your mind. This will help you in your studies of this Kua.

Strength Issuing Meditation:

Issue strength from the area of the upper back known as Ta Chu or "The Great Pillar." Envision waves of subtle strength radiating to all parts of your bodymind from this area.

CANTO # 40 — HSIEN/JIE

Rest/Ease/Lighten

An untamed storm of thunder and heavy rain
Reveals the mysterious gate of paradise.
If action is early and certain,
You may move forward by retreating
To a familiar and comfortable place.

MUSING WORDS:

**Clarify, Remove, Cut, Ox, Pare away,
Pointing, Clouds, Carpe diem/Seize the day**

HIDDEN HEXAGRAM: #63

MYSTIC WINDOW

Now is the time to take a break, relax, and recharge. The energy of problem solving is easily accessible. Above all, stay peaceful and calm while looking within for clues to improving yourself. But remember to employ a light hand and be gentle with your life and personal sensibilities. Extend a helping hand to a friend today.

Alchemic Wisdom
Yao Tsi (Line Verse):

1) Embrace the Qi of openness and surrender
To the Tao Source
And there will be no mistake or omission.

2) Three fox spirits appear in the field of
awareness.
An earth-seeking arrow finds the yellow center.
The signs are clear;
Embrace the unseen Qi of the spirit-realm
And abundance abounds.

3) Embrace the Qi of
Balance, poise, and equilibrium
Or thieves will come to rob you.
Be authentic or
You will have cause for sorrow.

4) Relax, sink to the earth, extend your Qi,
And the sincere and like-minded
Will be attracted to you.
Praise!

5) The elevated man is burdened by choice.
Abundance abounds for all.
Lower men can relax and feel confident.

6) The regal hunter looks up and spies his prey.
He picks his target carefully
And shoots his arrow.
His prize will fall from the city wall.
Press your advantage wisely.

Heaven and Earth Meditation:

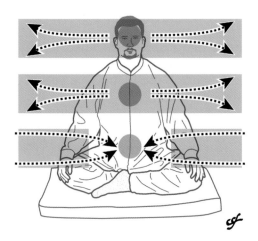

Mind Focusing Meditation:

The earthly energies that flow through your bodymind should be gathered at the back of your left hand. Rest a portion of your mind on this area.

Strength Issuing Meditation:

Issue strength from your Upper Tan Tien as you intuitively investigate the mysteries of this hexagram. This spot is located between the eyebrows, just above the nose and inward one inch from the surface of the skin.

Condense/Lessen/Quell

A lake joining the mountain at its base
Forms a partnership of change and repose.
Offering a sacrifice of food and wine
Paints a picture of two friends sitting in
silence.

MUSING WORDS:

**Pour out, Reach, Wine, Center, Lean, Loss,
Repose, Sacrificial ritual, Surrender**

HIDDEN HEXAGRAM: #24

MYSTIC WINDOW

It is best to give up any hard-lined opinions that you might have. Find a compromise position and middle path, particularly when encountering the problems of others. Observe events with an eye towards maintaining an overview of salient facts. Avoid crowds and over-stimulating circumstances.

Alchemic Wisdom
Yao Tsi (Line Verse):

1) Personal affairs desperately need tending to;
   Waste no time in addressing them.
   Embrace the Qi of simplicity.
   Remember, less is more.

2) Now is the time to consult the oracle.
   Turn inward and listen to your soul.
   Abundance gathers.
   Now is not the time to assault your enemy.
   It will only make him stronger.

3) Traveling alone requires too much Qi.
   Traveling with two companions is too frantic.
   It exhausts the Qi.
   Traveling with one companion
   Balances the journey.

4) Sending a message of warmest regards
Increases wellness
And puts disease to route.
It is not a mistake to spread happiness.

5) The Qi of longevity and abundance abounds
In the presence of thoughtful gifts.
It soothes the heartmind
And elevates the soul.

6) Go forward and acquire
Many people who will help you.
Revel in the Qi of abundance.
Now is not the time to pare down.

Heaven and Earth Meditation:

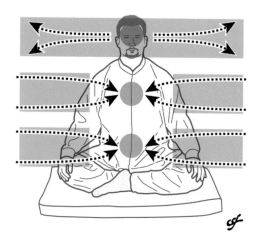

Mind Focusing Meditation:

Rest a portion of your mind on the palm of your right hand. This is an area of gathering and focus. Allow your will, thought, and imagination to collect there.

Strength Issuing Meditation:

When intuitively investigating this hexagram, issue strength from the area on the bodymind known as the Window Of The Sky. Also known as Tien Ch'uang, this area is located in and around the base of your skull.

Expand/Intensify/Excite

The power of the wind is supported by the
sounds of thunder.
Great journeys always begun with simple
steps,
Tell us to confidently cross the great stream
And penetrate the moment like an arrow.

MUSING WORDS:

**Increase, Chariot, Learned man or woman,
Gradually, Headwind, Heartmind, Riches**

HIDDEN HEXAGRAM: #23

MYSTIC WINDOW

Now is the time to avoid insincerity and selfishness. The energy of change beckons you to get moving, without delay. Do not become distressed or disheartened even if situations seem ominous or desperate. Stay upbeat. If you maintain a compassionate and optimistic disposition, then you will succeed.

Alchemic Wisdom
Yao Tsi (Line Verse):

1) Taking advantage of unfortunate circumstances
   And the misfortune of others
   Will be very profitable.
   Hard work accomplishes much.
   Embrace the Qi of confident determination.

2) The greatest gift is continuous insight
   Into the inner workings of men.
   The king offers thankful sacrifices
   To the Tao Source of life.

3) Take advantage of unfortunate circumstances
   And there will be no mistake.
   Walk from the Lower Heaven with confidence
   And keep to the centered Tao path.
   Influence brings abundance.

4) Follow the middle path
And influence follows.
Moving the seat of power and authority
Creates advantageous Qi.
Trust the relocation.

5) A kind heartmind is sincere.
A compassionate heartmind is uplifting.
Do not question the arrival of abundance.
Rather, keep to excellent exceptionalism.

6) A man's reach should exceed his grasp.
But only if he has a peaceful heartmind.
Without the restraint of peace
He will suffer a loss of abundance.

Heaven and Earth Meditation:

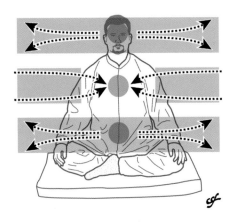

Mind Focusing Meditation:

Rest a portion of your mind on your left firmly closed fist. This is your point of focus during your exploration of the forty-second hexagram.

Strength Issuing Meditation:

Support your intuitive investigation into this hexagram by issuing strength from the Gateway of Life. Also known as the Ming Men, this area is located in and around the lumbar region of the spine.

Steadfast/Resolute/Cleanse

The lake's heart rises to the heavens
Just as archer loosens his arrow skyward.
Cast aside doubt like a released arrow
Before the power of water overflows across
the land.

MUSING WORDS:

**Upright sword, Water, Dragon, Bravery,
Tiger, Banner, Just reward**

HIDDEN HEXAGRAM: #1

MYSTIC WINDOW

Avoid half-heartedness at all costs during this period. Do not force an outcome. The situation is still in the process of unfolding. Purchase necessary supplies and plan for the future. At the same time, do not be consumed by worry. Seek to move forward but avoid large gains and be satisfied with smaller victories.

Alchemic Wisdom
Yao Tsi (Line Verse):

1) Strength gathers at leg's end.
   Muster the Qi of setting out.
   Unable to triumph
   You will make mistakes.

2) A call to arms
   And complete preparations.
   The sentries are posted;
   Now we wait for the signal.
   Until then, remain calm.

3) Cruelty in the face and eyes
   Reveals the Qi of misery.
   The elevated man organizes and clarifies
   Then sets out on his own.

He will encounter winds and rains
That will dampen his spirit.
But, he will not misstep.

4) Vitality and will has been drained.
The Qi of acquiescence prevails.
Events control and pull you along.
There is no integrity in the wilderness
Of someone who is ruled
By situations.

5) There is too much Qi to be useful.
The mustard seed begins small
But soon chokes everything.
Embrace the Tao Source,
Balance the Qi,
Clear the field.

6) If you cannot talk with your soul,
How can you speak with other people?
If you cannot follow the signs,
The outcome will be unwelcome.

Heaven and Earth Meditation:

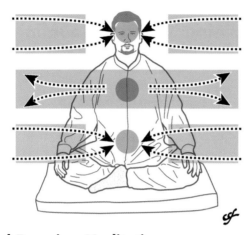

Mind Focusing Meditation:

Rest a portion of your mind on your closed left fist. This will help focus and rally the energy needed to unlock the mysteries of hexagram forty-three.

Strength Issuing Meditation:

Issue strength for the intuitive investigation from the area of the breastbone known as the Central Altar. This will support and invigorate your endeavors.

Joining/Contact/Coupling

Issuing from heaven
A continuous wind blows across the land.
Only a woman of stature and uncommon
strength
Can resist the tempest.

MUSING WORDS:

**Voluptuous, Queen, Intercourse,
Communicate, Drawn bow, Compose verse,
Blue-green (color)**

HIDDEN HEXAGRAM: #1

A malevolent force is trying to gain a foothold in your life. It is vital to meet it squarely with resoluteness. Rely upon assistance of a small group of friends to put this evil to rout. Be sure to base your actions upon your higher ideals. Make contact with that which is bigger than yourself.

Alchemic Wisdom
Yao Tsi (Line Verse):

1) Stand still
   Like a metal stake driven
   Into the earth.
   Great abundance abounds.
   Moving against the centering Qi
   Brings about a fall.

2) The moment is pregnant
   With possibilities.
   Stay close to home,
   Stay comfortable,
   Embrace the Tao Source, and
   Seek the grace of solitude.

3) Events control you.
   There is great peril if
   You allow this to continue.

Sink your root
And there will be no slips or blunders.

4) The moment is barren
And devoid of possibilities.
Any miscalculation can occur.

5) In the absence of a lover
Embrace the fruits of mankind.
Cultivate music, poetry, and romantic wisdom.
Stretch upward to receive Heaven's kiss
And its grace will descend to you.

6) Seek union with another
And embrace the Qi of completion.
Seek union of the Yin and Yang
And sink the Jade Stalk.
You will not misstep.
Now is the time of copulation and congress.

Heaven and Earth Meditation:

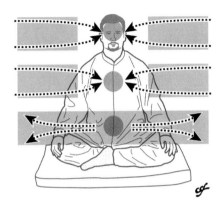

Mind Focusing Meditation:

Rest a portion of your mind on your breastbone and see all of your earthly energies collecting there. This includes your will, thought, vitality, and imagination.

Strength Issuing Meditation:

From the Gateway of Life, see subtle strength flowing to all points in the bodymind. This subtle strength is sometimes described as the "force of wisdom and sensitivity." It helps unlock the mysteries of the hexagram.

CANTO # 45 — TS'UI/CUI

Call Together/Assemble/Collect

A lake bird stands on one leg at the water's
edge,
As drum beats echo through the valley.
Moving waves blend effortlessly
With the still shoreline.

MUSING WORDS:

**Gather, Phoenix, Dragon, Polished jade,
Temple, Sacrificial offering, Flames**

HIDDEN HEXAGRAM: #53

MYSTIC WINDOW

It is time to pay homage to wisdom and experience. Focus your intent and keep your eye on the prize. Work alone but do not count on your past successes or reputation. Mindfully observe yourself as you work to accomplish your goals.

Alchemic Wisdom
Yao Tsi (Line Verse):

1) You are hearing words
But you cannot grasp the meaning.
Gather yourself and fortify your Qi.
Ask to hear the words again.
This time, listen simply.
Once the complex is made simple
You may relax and feel secure.

2) Allow abundance to lead you
And you will make no mistakes.
Allow the spirits to speak and sing to you
And more abundance will follow their music.

3) The Qi of disappointment presents itself.
You will feel heavy and slow.
Not fighting it brings sadness,
But no regrets.

4) The Qi of great abundance presents itself.
No problems, mistakes, or errors.

5) Consolidate your Qi by
Embracing the true breath.
Consolidate your spirit by
Embracing the Tao through ritual and music.
Your heartmind will clear.

6) Now is the time to mourn a loss.
Do not hide your grief.
Rather, find strength in it.

Heaven and Earth Meditation:

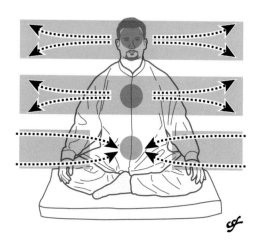

Mind Focusing Meditation:

Split your awareness between your breastbone and your right palm. Resting a portion of your mind on both areas, imagine that a gathering of energy, wisdom, and willpower takes place in each.

Strength Issuing Meditation:

As you intuitively explore this hexagram, support your endeavors by issuing subtle strength from the area of your crown known as the Palace of One Hundred Meetings.

CANTO # 46 — SHENG/SHENG

Rise/Conquer/Ascend

With earth above the promise of wood,
Growth on the mountain peak,
Like dust swept off a mirror's face,
Must persevere from seed to tree.

MUSING WORDS:

**Sunrise, Touchstone, Assess, Correct, Mirror,
Light rain, Portion out**

HIDDEN HEXAGRAM: #54

MYSTIC WINDOW

Now is the time to open lines of communication to mature growth. Slow and steady progress is the key. Do not exceed the basic goodness of consistency. Embrace righteousness and persistence. Know when to stop short as you advance forward. Above all, be cautious. If it seems too easy, then it cannot be trusted.

Alchemic Wisdom
Yao Tsi (Line Verse):

1) You are joining with the Tao Source.
   This signals abundance.
   Remain open, alert, and aware.
   Embrace quiet sincerity.

2) Put everything in its proper place
   And accept that the Qi of closure
   Will naturally approach.

3) Sounds and strange emanations
   Are rising upwards
   From a false and empty place.

4) A ruler reaches up and touches the sky.
　　Compassion is the hallmark,
　　Abundance is the goal.
　　The Tao Source reveals
　　The Tao Way of life.

5) When the soul beckons
　　Rise up to meet it
　　With deliberate steps and gestures.
　　Abundance abounds.

6) Deliberate steps and gestures
　　That answers the beckoning soul,
　　Push back the darkness.
　　Embrace the upright Qi of virtue.

Heaven and Earth Meditation:

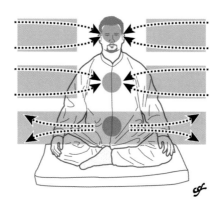

Mind Focusing Meditation:

Rest a portion of your mind on your breastbone.
Envision life force energy within and without
gathering to this area.

Strength Issuing Meditation:

During all of your investigations into the deeper
mysteries of this hexagram, it is best to issue
strength from the Lower Tan Tien. This is an energy
gathering spot located three and one-half inches
below your navel and inward towards the physical
center of your bodymind.

Enclose/Confine/Exhaust

Lake energy over water clogs the wheel,
Confines life, and ends growth.
Empty words exhaust life,
Surround the kingdom, and
Foretell defeat.

MUSING WORDS:

**Oppress, Dry river bed, Medicinal herbs,
Sickness, Open mouth, Trapped**

HIDDEN HEXAGRAM: #37

Alchemic Wisdom
Yao Tsi (Line Verse):

1) Punished and chastised,
   You enter into a dark and strange place.
   You will move about bereft and alone.

2) Abundance threatens those
   Who would control others.
   Follow the rules and order of things
   And do not press the issue
   Or draw attention to yourself.
   Listen to your soul.

3) You are trapped inside yourself.
   Your spirit is disturbed.
   Friend and foe look the same.

4) Move forward slowly and deliberately.
   Confusion and sorrows will vanish.

5) Those who would control others
   Will wrongfully accuse you of false crimes.
   Be authentic and cultivate the Tao.
   Speak often with your soul.

6) Natural forces restrain and imprison.
   Your bodymind is trapped
   But your soul can move forward.
   Forget what is behind you and
   Project your spirit forward.

Heaven and Earth Meditation:

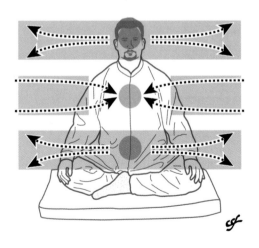

Mind Focusing Meditation:

Rest a portion of your mind on your left palm. See all of your energy, wisdom, and insight gathering there. You will need a focused bodymind to solve the mysteries of this hexagram.

Strength Issuing Meditation:

Issue strength from the Gateway of Life and you will intuitively become aware of the complex inner workings described in this canto. This area supplies the psychic strength necessary to project the spirit out of the bodymind.

Welling Up/Restore/Release

The strength of water over the strength of
wind
Reveals a penetrating strength
That moves the water wheel
And replenishes the entire surroundings.

MUSING WORDS:

**Watering, Buoyant, Uplifted, Pearl of
immortality, Wealth, Priest, Blessing,
Drawn forth**

HIDDEN HEXAGRAM: #38

Alchemic Wisdom
Yao Tsi (Line Verse):

1) The well is old;
   The water is poisoned.
   Seek nourishment elsewhere.

2) The well is cracked;
   The water leaks out.
   Seek to repair it.

3) The well is disturbed;
   The water is brackish.
   It was repaired improperly.
   Seek wisdom and try again.

4) The well is solid and firm;
   The water has integrity.
   No problems are present.

5) The well is filled;
The water is cool and nourishing.

6) The well is young;
The water is vibrant and healthy.
It forms the life center
Of all that gather around it.

Heaven and Earth Meditation:

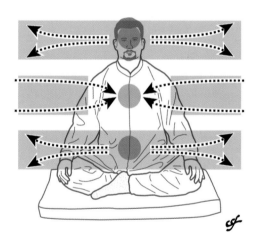

Mind Focusing Meditation:

Rest a portion of your mind on the palm of your opened left hand. This is the focusing point of your earthly energies. Fixing your gaze firmly upon this area will facilitate the necessary gathering of Qi.

Strength Issuing Meditation:

Issue strength from the Great Pillar or Ta Chu. This subtle strength will support your daily investigations into the mysteries of this hexagram.

Change/Shed/Revolve

The lake resting over fire
Portends a great change.
The patient turning of a great wheel
Reveals the depths hidden beneath the
surface.

MUSING WORDS:

**Hide, Skin, Dance, Hunt, Transform, Shaman,
Tiger, Banner**

HIDDEN HEXAGRAM: #44

MYSTIC WINDOW

It is time to listen to your imagination; the muse is speaking. Can you hear it? Engage in quiet contemplation today. Plan your actions carefully and position yourself accordingly. Watch your back and be open to the force of change.

Alchemic Wisdom
Yao Tsi (Line Verse):

1) Embrace the animal powers.
   Enter the yellow earth through the center
   And retrieve your inner strength.

2) Change your perspective.
   Resolutely tread a new path
   And the Qi of abundance will appear,
   Brushing aside problems of all kinds.

3) Stop!
   Do not proceed.
   There is danger ahead.
   Consider the signs,
   Consult with your soul and
   Alter your course with confidence.

4) Exude strength, optimism, and confidence.
Walk as if drawn forward by your soul
And you can change the will of heaven.

5) Embrace the Qi of transformation.
Be tenacious and strong like a tiger.
Consult the Tao,
Consult the soul.
The eight worlds are before you.

6) Embrace earthen Qi and transform yourself
To fit the moment.
Elevated men authentically adapt and change.
Lesser men just pretend.
Stop and consider your course of action.
Speak with your soul.

Heaven and Earth Meditation:

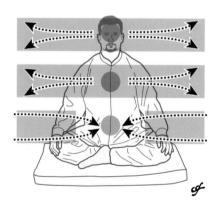

Mind Focusing Meditation:

Rest your attention on the back of your right hand and see it as a focal point for your physical and mental powers.

Strength Issuing Meditation:

Issue strength from the Upper Tan Tien. This will give you the insight necessary to decipher the wisdom contained in this canto. The Upper Tan Tien is located between the eyebrows, just above the nose and inward one inch from the surface of the skin.

Cauldron/Foothold/Offering

A wind flowing beneath the flames
Stokes the sacrificial fires
While appeasing the ancestors
And refining the golden elixir.

MUSING WORDS:

**Fearless, Sword, Sacrificial urn, Full moon,
Caution, Young man, Clouds, Continuity**

HIDDEN HEXAGRAM: #43

MYSTIC WINDOW

Give a gift of art or beauty to someone close to you. Now is the time to devise new pains born out of the desire for elegant solutions. This is a good time to clean house both emotionally and intellectually. Listen to your intuition and use your imagination to shape your intent and actions.

Alchemic Wisdom
Yao Tsi (Line Verse):

1) Lower the crucible
   To the Golden Elixir Field of Cinnabar.
   What was right and correct,
   Is now wrong and incorrect.
   Behave accordingly.
   Sacrifice to the spirits of your ancestors.

2) The crucible overflows
   And I possess wellness
   Unexpected by my adversaries.
   Great abundance abounds.

3) The crucible's handles are broken;
   It cannot be used.
   The rain will wash away
   The mess you've made of things.
   When the rains end,
   Abundance abounds.

4) The crucible's feet are broken
And the elixir within is wasted.
This brings catastrophe.

5) A strong man who can hear the earth,
See the winds, and
Shape the procession,
Will consult his soul
To reveal his riches.

6) The crucible is adorned
With the Dragon's essence.
Great abundance abounds.
This is the best of all possible times.

Heaven and Earth Meditation:

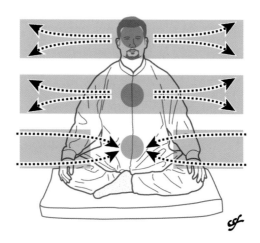

Mind Focusing Meditation:

Divide your attention between your spine and your lower back when studying the wisdom of this canto. This will help alter your consciousness enough to understand the hidden secrets.

Strength Issuing Meditation:

Issue strength from your Lower Tan Tien to support your investigations into the inner workings of this canto. The Lower Tan Tien is located three and one-half inches below your navel and inward towards the physical center of your bodymind.

CANTO # 51 —
CHEN/ZHEN

Seize/Initiate/Excite

Waves of rolling thunder
Call men to immediate action,
Splitting bamboo and wood
While embracing the dragon.

MUSING WORDS:

**Tremble, Thunderclap, Hidden, Impending,
Book, Treasure, Authority, Cloudburst,
Shockwave**

HIDDEN HEXAGRAM: #39

MYSTIC WINDOW

The energy of unusual things is present. Now is not the time to be sedate or listless. Instead, seize the moment and find unique paths to walk. Move forward "without hurry and without worry." Stay calm even in the face of difficulty.

Alchemic Wisdom
Yao Tsi (Line Verse):

1) A sudden clap of thunder
Startles and surprises.
It clears and loosens the spirit.
It ushers in ease and longevity.
Words flow easily into the silent night.
Abundance abounds.

2) Thunder brings shaking and the sounds of
danger.
Rest the heartmind in silence and solitude.
Embrace the Qi of openness and surrender.
Walk slowly through the Nine Palaces
And you will find contentment in seven days.

3) The sounds of danger make you nervous.
Proceed even if your strength is bravado.
Everything will be fine.

4) Thunder confuses the heartmind.
Wait until the heartmind clears
Before moving on.

5) Be brave as the danger comes and goes.
Even now things can move forward.

6) A murder of crows frames the sounds of thunder.
Clear the channels by looking left and right.
Gather the Qi.
Still the bodymind must not move forward.
To move will bring calamity.

Heaven and Earth Meditation:

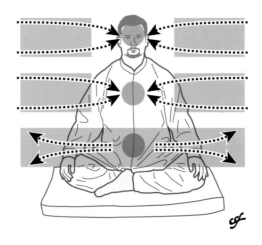

Mind Focusing Meditation:

Rest a portion of your mind upon your breastbone as you study this canto. Imagine that an invisible hand is gently resting upon it.

Strength Issuing Meditation:

Issue strength from your Lower Tan Tien as you seek to intuitively understand the "ins and outs" of this canto.

CANTO # 52 — KEN/GEN

Release/Still/Sedate

Mountain above and mountain below,
Reveals energy that must pause at the gate
Before the gentleman becomes a sage,
Frees the self, and achieves immortality.

MUSING WORDS:

Monkey, Three (3), Spine, Mirror, Courtyard, Anxious

HIDDEN HEXAGRAM: #40

Now is the time to think before you speak and think even longer before taking action. Take a step back and assess the situation carefully. Embrace quietude and stillness both internally and externally. Be still and closely examine all of your options. This is a great time to learn to meditate.

Alchemic Wisdom
Yao Tsi (Line Verse):

1) The feet are as sedate as mountains.
Thus stilled,
The soul walks without misstep.

2) The legs are as sedate as mountains.
Thus stilled,
The heartmind is upset and no help is
   forthcoming.

3) The loins are as sedate as mountains.
Thus stilled,
The heartmind becomes frantic and self-
   destructive.

4) The bodymind is as sedate as mountains.
The soul travels about on its own.
The Five Elements are balanced
And the emotions are stable.

5) The mouth is as sedate as mountains.
The right words can be said.
The Qi of regrets dissipates.

6) Be as sedate as mountains
With the soul as active as a raging river.
Stillness begets authenticity and
Authenticity begets stillness.
Abundance abounds.

Heaven and Earth Meditation:

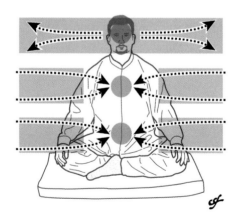

Mind Focusing Meditation:

Rest a portion of your mind on your left shoulder joint. Focus all of your gifts and deficits to this part of your bodymind. Consider the *I Ching* aphorism that, "wisdom comes from the left."

Strength Issuing Meditation:

Support your search for wisdom in this canto by issuing strength from the Gateway of Life. Also known as the Ming Men, this area is located in and around the lumbar area of the spine.

Headwaters/Advance/Slowly

The wind blows low over the mountaintops
In small steps that become great strides.
From a lofty vantage point,
All things look new and small.

MUSING WORDS:

**Glide, Float, Ascend, Watchtower, Cauldron,
Wild goose, Timberline, Bottomland, Young
growth**

HIDDEN HEXAGRAM: #64

MYSTIC WINDOW

Now is the time to be aware of what others are saying about you. Be it praise or malicious gossip, listen dispassionately and try to determine what is really being said "between the lines." Obstacles are a natural part of advancement. Do not be bothered by them. Be thankful for what you have already accomplished.

Alchemic Wisdom
Yao Tsi (Line Verse):

1) Slander, gossip, and excessive speech
   Damages the young soul.
   Avoid them in order to avoid mistakes.
   A wild goose flies to the shore.

2) Seek the Qi
   Of pleasure, nourishment, food, and drink.
   Be happy, optimistic, and joyful.
   A wild goose lands on a large rock.

3) Seek the Qi
   Of nourishment, safety, and comfort.
   Protect yourself from the calamities that
      approach.
   A wild goose approaches barren land.

4) Seek the Qi
Of completion to obtain success
And there will be no miscalculation.
A wild goose flies toward treetops.

5) Seek the Qi
Of stability, strength, and acceptance
And all things will rest in peace.
Abundance will abound.
A wild goose lands on an ancestral tomb.

6) Seek the Qi
Of ritual, music, and poetry
And rest within the heartbeat of the Tao.
A wild goose rests on dry land.

Heaven and Earth Meditation:

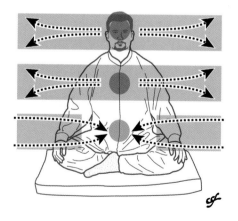

Mind Focusing Meditation:

As you study the wisdom of this canto, divide your attention between your spine and middle back. Resting a portion of your mind on these areas will facilitate a gathering of natural energy in your bodymind.

Strength Issuing Meditation:

Issue strength from your Lower Tan Tien. This will support your intuitive investigations into the fifty-third canto. This energy loci is located three and one-half inches below your navel and inward towards the physical center of your bodymind.

CANTO # 54 — KUEI
MEI/GUI MEI

Culminate/Marry/Arrive

The sounds of thunder over the lake
Reveal a sun threatened and obscured by
clouds.
The procession must stop, hold its ground,
And celebrate where they stand.

MUSING WORDS:

**Wedding party, Self-sufficient, Stumble,
Herald, Great literature, Broom**

HIDDEN HEXAGRAM: #63

The energy of a developing situation has exhausted itself. Now is the time to stop and celebrate your accomplishments even if your achievement is only a small one. Moving forward at this time will only bring misfortune and bad luck. Expect delays, but don't worry about them.

Alchemic Wisdom
Yao Tsi (Line Verse):

1) Accept a lesser role and
   Embrace the Qi of assisting
   Rather than of leading.

2) Sometimes,
   Only a blind man can see the truth.
   Be blind;
   Consult the soul.

3) Accept a position of partial leadership.
   Embrace the Qi of co-operation
   Rather than of contention.

4) Now is the time to
Embrace patient Qi
And wait to see what happens naturally.
Everything has its own time of ripening.

5) Look to the Yin moon
For wisdom and contentment.
Absorb the moon essence.
Absorb the moon spirit.

6) An offering already burnt
Will bring no abundance.
A barren womb
Will produce no children.
These are inauspicious times.

Heaven and Earth Meditation:

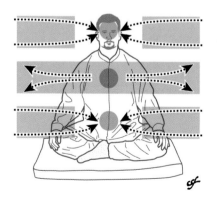

Mind Focusing Meditation:

Rest a portion of your mind on your back and spine. Envision your energy, will, and vitality gathering there.

Strength Issuing Meditation:

Issue strength from the area of your upper back known as the "Great Pillar." Subtle strength radiates from this area as you intuitively investigate the relevance of this hexagram in your life.

Bountiful/Teeming/Plenty

Fire lightning rumbles through the clouds,
Yet the sun shines upon the sacrifice
As its power is focused,
Revealing an abundance of life force.

MUSING WORDS:

**Full, Abundant, Joyful sounds, Dragon, Tiger,
Snake, A new day, Noon, Eclipse, Focus**

HIDDEN HEXAGRAM: #28

MYSTIC WINDOW

Above all, be humble at this time. Give thanks for what has been produced by your efforts by returning something to the community you serve. Share your good fortune. Now is not the time to be alone. Rely on teamwork and people who share your vision and goals.

Alchemic Wisdom
Yao Tsi (Line Verse):

1) See your equal in the ten days
   Of cooperative effort
   And no mistakes occur.
   Move forward to an end.
   Much praise is in order.

2) Make yourself invisible.
   Absorb the Qi of the Great Dipper
   And Pole Star.
   Stand on one leg and pause
   Before proceeding confidently onward.
   Carry the Qi of the Tao Source with you.
   Abundance abounds.

3) The Qi flows abundantly.
Absorb the Qi of Arcturus
And project balanced will.
Night becomes day,
Day becomes night.

4) Make yourself invisible.
Absorb the Qi of the Great Dipper
At noontime
And you will please the king
As you rest the heartmind.

5) The pages of eternity
Will turn in your favor.
Great abundance awaits.

6) He is invisible even to himself.
How sad!
He is alone.
People walk by but no one sees him.
How unfortunate.

Heaven and Earth Meditation:

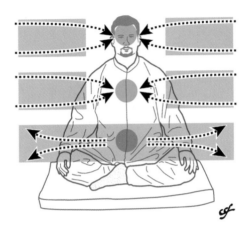

Mind Focusing Meditation:

Rest a portion of your mind on your middle and upper back. See these areas as gathering points for your earthly energies such as your will, thought, and imagination.

Strength Issuing Meditation:

Issue strength for your intuitive investigations from the Central Altar area of your breastbone. This will accelerate your intuitive understanding of the hexagram.

CANTO # 56 — LU/LU

Explore/Travel/Take Flight

Fires on the mountain
Signal an impending sacrifice and pitched battle.
Embrace the ordered way of things and
Traverse the wilderness
As life and death give chase.

MUSING WORDS:

Dance, Frenzy, Campfires, Lucky star, Three (3), Hardship, Mischief, Being chased

HIDDEN HEXAGRAM: #28

MYSTIC WINDOW

Now is not the time for a nuanced view of life.
If you think too much, you will become bogged
down in minutiae. That having been said, plan
your travels carefully and rely upon your
intuition to guide you. Get moving! Staying in
one place brings misfortune.

Alchemic Wisdom
Yao Tsi (Line Verse):

1) A loathsome visitor is approaching.
Protect yourself.

2) Behave as an honorable and respectful traveler
Wherever you go.
Upon breaking camp
Leave the place better than you found it.

3) The campsite is burnt and unusable.
Danger is afoot.
Move cautiously to another site.

4) If you camp alone in the wilderness
Who will keep watch?
No rest.
No safety.
The heartmind is disturbed.

5) A meal in the wilderness
Can be costly of effort, arrows, and time.
Yet, the Tao Source provides.

6) When the camp is ablaze
Everything is lost in the confusion.
The traveler laughs hysterically
From grief.

Heaven and Earth Meditation:

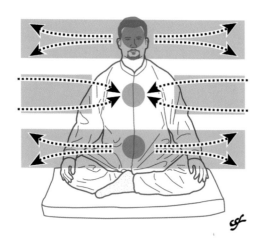

Mind Focusing Meditation:

Rest a portion of your mind on the palm of the right hand. This is your gathering point for the will, thought, and imagination.

Strength Issuing Meditation:

Issue strength from the Ta Chu or "Great Pillar" to support your intuitive investigations into this canto.

CANTO # 57 — SUN/XUN

Gentle/Wind/Penetrate

Winds above and winds below
Are unseen, tenacious, and resolute.
Effortlessly blend your heartmind accordingly
And be
Unseen, tenacious, and resolute.

MUSING WORDS:

**Joyful song, Partnership, Join, Two (2),
Snakes, Clouds, Archer, To enter, Seep**

HIDDEN HEXAGRAM: #38

MYSTIC WINDOW

Now is not the time for prevarication, squeamishness, or passivity. In all of your actions, behave resolutely and single-mindedly. Be cautious, but stand your personal ground. People with ulterior motives will try to take advantage of you. Push back their negative influences with quiet contemplation and mindful activity.

Alchemic Wisdom
Yao Tsi (Line Verse):

1) Wind can move forward or backward.
   The warrior consults his soul
   And the wise general.
   Then, he proceeds with confidence and
      purpose.

2) An ill wind moves beneath the bed
   Signaling a need to consult a magician.
   Where is the precise congress of heaven and
      earth?
   What does it say?
   Find out and abundance abounds.

3) A strong wind blows too long
   And brings sorrows and regrets.

4) The wind subsides enough
   To capture three different kinds of birds.
   There is auspicious variety in the field.

5) The wind's end is a beginning.
   The wind's beginning is an end.
   The Qi will shift mid-week.
   If the dictates of the soul are
   Heard and heeded
   Abundance will abound.

6) An ill wind moves beneath the bed.
   No rest.
   No safety.
   A thief has taken it all.
   This is very unfortunate.

Heaven and Earth Meditation:

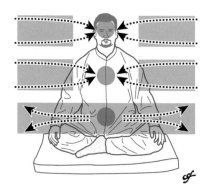

Mind Focusing Meditation:

Rest a portion of your mind on the palm of your right hand. This is your point of mental focus. Use it to clear and quiet your mind.

Strength Issuing Meditation:

Issue strength from the Central Altar. The subtle force emanating from this area is your motive force for the actions suggested by this canto.

CANTO # 58 — TUI/DUI

Pleasure/Joy/Rest

Lake above and lake below
Gives birth to the spirit of the dance
And the voice of song.
Stand upright within the heart of the moment.

MUSING WORDS:

**Union, Yoke, Wedding, Speak, Laughter,
Moonrise, Smile**

HIDDEN HEXAGRAM: #37

MYSTIC WINDOW

It is the time to rest and enjoy the moment. Do not get bogged down in the minutiae of life. Maintain an optimistic and relaxed view of your day-to-day activities and rely upon your intuition to guide your actions. Trust only close friends today. Now is the time to identify with and indulge in deep pleasure.

Alchemic Wisdom
Yao Tsi (Line Verse):

1) Embrace the Qi of deep pleasure.
Harmonize your inner and outer worlds.
Abundance abounds.

2) Embrace the Qi of deep pleasure.
Be confident, brave, and upright.
Abundance abounds and worries vanish.

3) Now is not the time to identify
With deep pleasure.
Embrace the Qi of pragmatism and duty.

4) Do not obsess about being pleased and happy.
When deep pleasure presents itself
It will be the right time to indulge.
Help it into existence.

5) Stay where you are
And keep the high ground.
Danger appears when confidence falters.

6) Follow your own path
And not someone else's.
Soon there will be abundance.

Heaven and Earth Meditation:

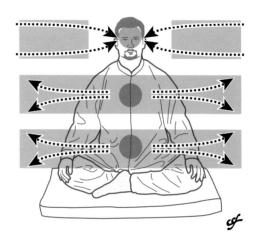

Mind Focusing Meditation:

Rest a portion of your mind on the palm of your closed left hand. Gather all of your earthly forces in this area as a means of consolidating the energy of intuitive investigation. Apply this energy to deciphering the secrets of the Kua.

Strength Issuing Meditation:

Issue the strength for your intuitive investigations from the area known as the Gateway of Life. Remember, this subtle strength shapes and motivates all of your actions when exploring the hexagram.

CANTO # 59 — HUAN/HUAN

Dissipate/Spread/Water

A strong wind blowing over the lake
Is heaven's way
Of spreading the temple's energy
Across the land
So each may go their separate way.

MUSING WORDS:

Flood, Knife, Shaman, Float downstream, Following, Seclusion, Temple, Flotsam and jetsam

HIDDEN HEXAGRAM: #27

MYSTIC WINDOW

Be wary of the energy of dissolution, but know that the fog will soon lift. Now is the time to operate from a place of abundance. Contribute to a charity, help others, drop a bad habit, and eliminate confusion from your life. Now is the time to visit your church and lean upon your faith.

Alchemic Wisdom
Yao Tsi (Line Verse):

1) Have no fear;
   Help is on the way.
   Embrace the Qi of patience and hope.

2) Quickly!
   Stand still and stretch out to the four corners.
   Keep to the center.
   Use whatever devices are available
   To help you connect with the life around you.
   Regrets will disappear and worries vanish.

3) Expand your soul
   And there will be no problems.

4) Qi expands;
   Qi contracts.
   The oscillations cannot be forced
   But will move freely throughout the land.

5) The king demands a sacrifice of human energy.
   Doing as he wants will eliminate mistakes.

6) Scatter the blood that binds you
   To your past.
   This dispersion signals a new beginning.

Heaven and Earth Meditation:

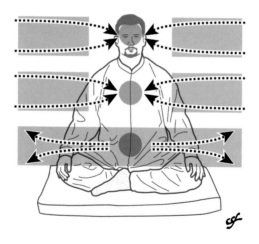

Mind Focusing Meditation:

Rest a portion of your mind on your right, open, and upturned palm. Imagine that it becomes light and buoyant as your earthly energies gather there.

Strength Issuing Meditation:

Issue strength from the area in and around the base of your skull known as the Window of the Sky. This will facilitate the state of consciousness necessary to penetrate the deep mysteries of the fifty-ninth canto.

Limit/Save/Regulate

Flood waters in the lake
Are held in check by its banks.
The life around it is divided
Like a bamboo fortress.

MUSING WORDS:

**Hold in check, Curb, Good news, Escape,
High ground, Placid, Govern**

HIDDEN HEXAGRAM: #27

MYSTIC WINDOW

Today is the day to keep to familiar surroundings. Do not spend capriciously or exhaust yourself physically or emotionally. In all areas, observe restraint. Now is the time for adopting a new set of rules and regulations.

Alchemic Wisdom
Yao Tsi (Line Verse):

1) Embrace the Qi of stillness and solitude.
   Do not leave the confines
   Of your home
   And no mistakes will be made.

2) Embrace the Qi of action and awareness.
   Leave the confines of your home and land
   Or there will be disaster.

3) No rules applied or followed
   Elicits melancholy and torpor.
   Yet, "no action" means "no mistakes."

4) Simple and elegant rules
   Make for a peaceful awakening.
   Seek the oracle.
   Make a sacrifice of human energy.

5) Pleasant rules, easily followed,
Bring abundance.
Proceed in the shape of metal
And you will be praised.

6) Unpleasant rules, difficult to ignore,
Break the spirit
As they lead you to disaster.
They are an ill wind
That cannot blow forever.

Heaven and Earth Meditation:

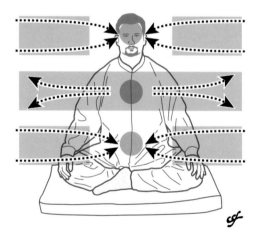

Mind Focusing Meditation:

Rest a portion of your mind on your back and spine. Gather your energy in these areas as if you are drawing a bow.

Strength Issuing Meditation:

Issue strength from the Great Pillar area of your upper back. This will support all of your investigations into the mysteries of this canto.

CANTO # 61 — CHUNG FU/ZHONG FU

Trust/Centered/Truth

The lake bird lands on the lake's edge
And calls out for all to hear.
With one leg raised and wings spread,
It rests on the breeze.

MUSING WORDS:

Confident, Bull's eye, Sincerity, Inner, Egg yolk, Dedicate, Authentic, Goose, Deer, Town crier

HIDDEN HEXAGRAM: #27

MYSTIC WINDOW

Now is the time for heartfelt sincerity. Have the courage and fortitude to be yourself. Living up to the image others have of you will not be advantageous at this time. Be true to yourself.

Alchemic Wisdom
Yao Tsi (Line Verse):

1) Embrace the Qi of solitude
   And the wisdom of repose.
   Alone, you are abundant.
   With others you will be sparse.

2) Reach out with your Qi
   And fortify what is in front of you.
   Harmonize your inner family
   And share your gifts.

3) Confused and uncertain Qi
   Gathers around you.
   Should you sing or keep silent?
   Do you beat a drum or remain seated?
   Frozen action brings great sadness.

4) The receptive Yin is almost at hand.
Squeeze the capsule and change directions.
Exercise freedom of choice
And you choose freedom.

5) The Qi of sincerity attracts the Qi of life.
There will be no missteps.

6) Your will dissipates
As your spirit becomes thin and airy.
There is calamity as far as the crow flies.

Heaven and Earth Meditation:

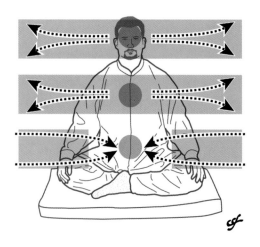

Mind Focusing Meditation:

Divide your awareness between your breastbone and left open palm. Both of these areas should be seen as gathering points of energy, will, and imagination. Gently rest a portion of your mind on each.

Strength Issuing Meditation:

Strength should be issued from the area on your bodymind known as the Palace of One Hundred Meetings. Also known as the Pai Hui, this is the strength of the Eternal Tao flowing into the crown of your head.

Humble/Ordinary/Beyond

The lake bird soars high
Above the thunder and mountaintops.
It plunges to the lake
And spears a fish.

MUSING WORDS:

**Small, Gentle, Advancement, Full moon,
Palace guard, Gate, Doorway, Freed,
Bird call, Sea bottom, Great ocean**

HIDDEN HEXAGRAM: #28

Today is the day to be watchful and prepared. You will have to take quick action when needed. Now is the time to go with your strengths. Stop short and don't fill to the brim. Do not press for a resolution to any problem. Stay relaxed, humble, and understated.

Alchemic Wisdom
Yao Tsi (Line Verse):

1) Look up and watch the birds
   Flying high in the sky.
   They follow the shape of the Dragon's tail.
   Their pattern of flight
   Reveals an ill omen.
   Have great care,
   Sink your root.
   Seek the Qi of nourishment.

2) Enter the spirit-realm
   And move forward,
   Leaving home and family behind.
   Move past lesser spirits
   And seek the ghost of order over chaos.
   Embrace a controlled heartmind
   And no mistakes will occur.

3) Do not leave the sacred space
To chase an angry ghost into the woods.
It is a trap!
His spear will turn on you.

4) The demon and his discontent stand before you.
It is no use to avoid it.
Cautiously meet it face-to-face.
The time for petition and negotiation is over.

5) Embrace the endless Qi of unlimited possibilities
Allowing it to flow through you.
Embrace the spirit of intuition
As you hunt the forest for herbs and medicines.

6) Birds flying high in the sky.
A broken bow pulled past its limits.
Things have gone too far
And you are alone in the demon-realm.
This signals catastrophe.

Heaven and Earth Meditation:

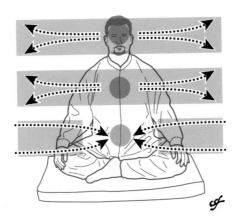

Mind Focusing Meditation:

Rest a portion of your mind on your left down-turned palm. Imagine that the gathering earthly energies make your whole hand heavy. Your hand seeks the earth.

Strength Issuing Meditation:

Issue strength from the Window of the Sky. Remember, all of your motive force for action or contemplation comes from this area located in and around the base of your skull.

CANTO # 63 — CHI CHI JI JI

Finished/Not Ended/Moving

Fire moving beneath the water
Reveals itself as subtle energy upon the surface
That has not yet exhausted itself.
It remains muted and fine-drawn.

MUSING WORDS:

Kneeling, Last course, Rainstorm, Release, Time, Ford a river, Conclude, Two children, Ultimate

HIDDEN HEXAGRAM: #64

MYSTIC WINDOW

Now is the time to celebrate an ending. Remember, the energy of ending feeds yet another beginning. It is all part of a perpetual cycle. Act with self-discipline and control. Now is not the time to force activity. Exhibit sincerity, modesty, and humility, but do not surrender control to anyone.

Alchemic Wisdom
Yao Tsi (Line Verse):

1) Fear abounds.
   He reluctantly and slowly circles.
   Embrace the situation as it is.
   Enter deeply into the moment.
   Now is the time to wet your tail.

2) Now is not the time to search
   For treasure, jewels, and elixirs.
   Wait
   And they will find their way to you.

3) The elevated master enters the demon-realm
And slays the enemy
He finds there.
Embrace the Qi of victory.
The nattering and small-minded are useless
In the extreme.

4) Apply temporary repairs and proceed.
Reassess the situation at day's end.
Embrace the Qi of caution.

5) Of two men,
Who does heaven revere?
The authentic man moving in the field of
      possibilities
Is blessed under heaven.
The unauthentic man is not.
For he is barely a man.

6) You are swamped by the Qi of the moment.
Find the shore and cling to a rock.
Your head is very wet.

Heaven and Earth Meditation:

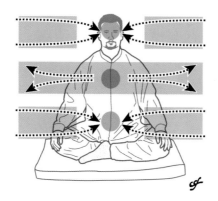

Mind Focusing Meditation:

Rest a portion of your mind on your closed right fist. This is your firm point of focus. It helps gather your mental powers for an investigation into the wonders of the canto.

Strength Issuing Meditation:

Issue strength from the Central Altar as you study this canto. Allow subtle force to flow from this point to all areas of your bodymind as you intuitively seek to discover the mysteries of the sixty-third hexagram.

Not-Finished/Ended/Moving

Fire dances on the water's surface
While treasures resting below
Remain hidden in plain sight.
A single drop of water
Will change everything.

MUSING WORDS:

**Penultimate, Next-to-last, Final gasp, Tiger,
Banners, Axe, Wind gust, Broadsword**

HIDDEN HEXAGRAM: #63

MYSTIC WINDOW

Now is not the time to overreach. Circumspection is the key to success as your situation is in flux. Be alert. If you see a problem, correct it resolutely and as quickly as possible. Don't get caught in the cusp of changing circumstances. Above all, trust your intuition and wait for the precise moment to react.

Alchemic Wisdom
Yao Tsi (Line Verse):

1) The changeling wets his fox-tail
   And is off balance.
   He has cause to regret his carelessness.

2) Move slowly and deliberately.
   Embrace the even Qi and
   Consult the soul.
   Abundance abounds.

3) This journey is not over yet.
   Cross the great stream
   But go no further.

4) Shake off the confusion like a horse
   Trembles and shakes off sweat.
   Seek nourishment, stand firm, and

Attack the demons where they live.
Abundance abounds.
Great success will approach you in threes.

5) Your soul will tell you
Whatever you need to do.
Listen and heed the messages.
Embrace authenticity,
Be creative,
Shine brightly, and
Feed your spirit.

6) Being just drunk enough
And not one bit more,
Brings freedom, strength, and confidence
Without mistakes of any kind.
Being just drunk enough
And a little bit more
Brings lassitude, weakness, bravado,
And unauthentic wisdom.
Embrace the Qi of authenticity.

Heaven and Earth Meditation:

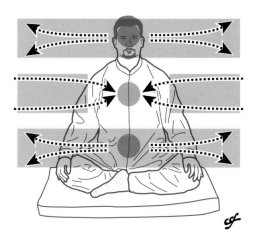

Mind Focusing Meditation:

Focus your gathering awareness on your Upper Tan Tien. This area is located between the eyebrows, just above the nose and inward one inch from the surface of the skin. Gently gather your thoughts, energies, and your willpower at this point. Combined with the following meditation, it will alter your consciousness so you will be ushered in to the heart of the sixty-fourth hexagram.

Strength Issuing Meditation:

As you are gathering your earthly powers to your Upper Tan Tien, you should issue subtle strength from your Lower Tan Tien. This is an energy gathering spot located three and one-half inches below your navel and inward towards the physical center of your bodymind. These two powerful meditations will sustain you in your cultivation of this Canto.

HEXAGRAM LOCATOR

Upper → Trigrams Lower ↓	Ch'ien	Chên	K'an	Kên	K'un	Sun	Li	Tui
Ch'ien	1	34	5	26	11	9	14	43
Chên	25	51	3	27	24	42	21	17
K'an	6	40	29	4	7	59	64	47
Kên	33	62	39	52	15	53	56	31
K'un	12	16	8	23	2	20	35	45
Sun	44	32	48	18	46	57	50	28
Li	13	55	63	22	36	37	30	49
Tui	10	54	60	41	19	61	38	58

ABOUT THE AUTHOR

Reverend John A. Bright-Fey is a philosopher, musician, and mystic, who has dedicated his life to preserving the world's vanishing oral literature. An accomplished Master of the Chinese healing and martial arts, he is the sole inheritor of more than two dozen privately held wisdom lineages. An ordained priest in the Buddhist and Taoist traditions, he is also the creator of the New Forest® Way, a groundbreaking paradigm that allows modern audiences greater access to the ancient wisdom traditions of India, China, and Tibet. John is the author of the *I Ching*, *Tao Te Ching*, and several books in the Whole Heart and Morning Cup series.

ABOUT THE CALLIGRAPHY

The characters used throughout this book are written in *Tien-Shu* Celestial Script. Each was spontaneously composed after a prolonged session of Ch'an/Zen contemplation that guided its creation. The author's seal chop with each character means, "primal act of creation in a mystic state."

Ch'an Hsing / Deeply Refining One's Nature

Notes:

Notes: